MW01128495

Abused to Death 4

Do Something

**Six more stories
of children murdered by
their parents or caregivers**

Jessica Jackson

This work is based on real cases
*The first part of each story is semi-fictionalised,
with some events and dialogue added*

*The second part tells the facts of each case,
detailing the injuries, trials and sentencing*

*For the purposes of anonymity, names of
siblings and friends have been changed
unless where commonly known*

*Cover photograph by
Annie Spratt at Unsplash
(posed by model)*

Contents

Thank You For Choosing This Book

Whether you're new to my books, or have been around since Volume 1, I'm truly thankful that you're reading my latest book.

But please proceed with caution if stories of murdered children are likely to deeply upset you.

> If you can spare a moment when you've finished reading, I'd be very grateful if you'd help me to raise awareness of child abuse by rating or reviewing this book.

I also have a FREE e-book for you.

You can check it out overleaf ...

Acknowledgments

With grateful thanks to:

- All my readers, including you – you keep me writing when the going gets tough

- My Beta Readers – Jackson, Linda and Rick

- My Advance Readers – I couldn't continue to write and raise awareness without you

- My Readers' List – your support and encouragement are priceless

- Robert Keller, Ryan Green and Jason Neal – thank you for continuing to promote my books to your own readers

- My Facebook followers – although I was anxious about joining (I'm not a social media whizz) you have increased my confidence and my presence – thank you so much

Your Free E-Book

Exclusive only to my readers

The tragic case
of Isaiah Torres

*(with bonus content about
Baby Brianna Lopez)*

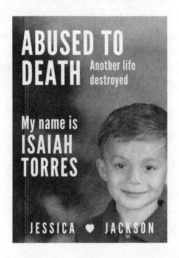

I'll let you know how to get your copy later

*(Royalties from my books go to
NSPCC, UNICEF and
Prevent Child Abuse America)*

This Volume

In this digital age, we often now have tangible proof, in the form of texts, social media, and graphic photographs, of the children's suffering. This is true for several children in this volume. But the last story, that of Adrian Jones, is considered by many to be the most horrific case imaginable, as we are able to view his abuse in video form. I can only hope that the changes made in Adrian's name will benefit children in the coming years.

My dream is to see an end to these hideous crimes, but until then, ABCD:

> A - Assume nothing
>
> B - Be vigilant
>
> C - Check everything
>
> D - Do something

And LISTEN to the children

The Playroom

(Dear Reader, please flip back for a message from the author, and your FREE ebook)

'Come on, kids. You can move your toys in here now.'

'But it smells, Mommy.'

'Not any more, honey, I've cleaned it up real good. It's going to be your new playroom. Look, I already brought your doll-house in here.'

'Isn't that boy coming back, Mommy?'

She crouches down. 'No, he's not coming back. Forget about him, okay? We don't talk about him anymore.'

'Did he go away?'

'Yes, yes he's gone away. And you mustn't think about him. Or tell anyone about him.'

'I couldn't tell much, Mommy, because I never really saw him.'

'That's right, honey. He was naughty and we had to keep him in here to punish him.'

'But when I'm naughty you just tell me not to do that again, or sometimes Daddy swats my butt.'

The woman smiles. 'I know, sweetheart. But he was very very naughty. He had to be punished a little more than that.'

'Where did he go, Mommy?'

'Far away, honey. Like I said, don't even think about him anymore, okay?'

'Okay, Mommy. I'll go bring my furniture for the doll-house.'

Nine Years Earlier

'Sit down, Max, for God's sake.'

'Wait to see Mommy.'

'She'll be here soon enough.'

'Me stay at window. Wait for Mommy.'

She snorts and looks at Daddy. 'He can't even talk properly.'

'Give the kid a break, Kim. He's only three.'

'Well, he gets on my nerves.'

'I know he does, babes. But while Sara's here, let's just get through it.'

'Why on earth did you invite her anyway?'

'She's his mom. And not a bad mom, really.'

'You're kidding me, right?'

'She's had a lot of bad luck, is all.'

'And now I'm stuck with her kid, and I have to pretend to like him.'

'It's just for one day.' He catches her round the waist. 'Hey, you've done a great job. That turkey looks fantastic.'

'I shouldn't be spending Thanksgiving with the brat's mom, that's all I'm saying.'

'Mommy here, Mommy here,' I shout.

'You'd better behave yourself, Max,' says Daddy. 'Be good for Daddy and Kim.'

'Be good,' I say, climbing down from the sofa and rushing to the door. 'Mommy, Mommy.'

She picks me up and kisses my cheeks. 'My little man. Oh, I've missed you.'

'Miss you, Mommy.'

'Hi, Scott. Hi, Kim. Thanks so much for having me visit.'

'That's okay,' says Kim.

'Hope you're hungry,' says Daddy.

'Always,' laughs Mommy. 'Now, I've got presents for everyone. Okay for me to give the kids theirs now?'

'You shouldn't have,' says Kim. 'But yes, that's real nice of you.'

Mommy reaches into her big bag, and my half-brothers and sisters and me gather round.

'Happy Thanksgiving,' says Mommy as she hands each of us a parcel.

A Year Later

'Everything still okay at Daddy's house, Max?'

'Yes,' I say. I don't want to tell Mommy that I got paddled a couple of times. 'But I like it here with you and my new Daddy more.'

'Oh, sweetheart, I wish you could come back and live with us. But the judge said Daddy could look after you better than me.'

'But now, Mommy? Now you have my new Daddy to take care of you?'

'I tried that, Max. Remember? And the judge said "No". We can still have lots of fun times together though, can't we? Like when you come visit like this.'

'We sure can.'

'We'll see how things go for a little while, and then we'll ask the judge again.' She lifts me onto her lap. 'Want to look at your book again?'

I nod. I love learning my ABC and my colours, and I point to each picture in turn as Mommy reads the words. 'Where's the apple? And what colour is it?'

Mom's boyfriend calls from the driveway. 'Come on, you guys. Don't you even *want* to go fishing?'

'We're coming,' calls Mommy, closing the book.

'Sometimes I dream that I live with you all the time, Mommy.'

She lifts me into her arms. 'Maybe one day, baby. Now how about we go catch some fish?'

'And the picnic,' I say. 'Don't forget about the picnic.'

'It was so nice at Mommy's today,' I tell my step-mom.

'Uh-uh,' says Kim.

'Daddy took us out in his jeep and we went fishing, and –'

My real Daddy jumps up out of the chair. 'Your what?'

'I mean, Mommy's boyfriend, Daddy.'

'I heard what you said, Max.'

'But I didn't mean it. I know *you're* my daddy. My real daddy.'

'Don't say his name in this house. You get me, Max?'

'Yes, Daddy. I won't say anything about him.' I pause. 'Mommy doesn't mind when I tell her about you and Kim-Mommy.'

Daddy thumps me upside the head. 'That's different. You live with us. You're with Kim every day. She's your mommy now.'

'Okay, Daddy. I'm really sorry.'

'Go to your room and stay there. No supper for you.'

I trudge up the stairs. I don't like it when Daddy or Kim are cross with me. They beat me and hurt me bad sometimes. I hope they don't stay mad for long.

As it starts to get dark, I go out of my room to use the bathroom before I go to sleep.

'Max!' Daddy roars at me as I'm on my way back across the hall. 'Did I tell you that you could leave your room? Did I?'

'No, Daddy. But I just went to use the bathroom.' He can't be mad at me for that.

'Oh well, that's okay then,' he says. 'Except that I *told* you to stay in your room.'

'I'm sorry, Daddy. I really needed to go.'

'Get back in there. And don't come out till I tell you.'

The next morning, I need the bathroom again. What do I do? It's for the big one this time, and I can't hold it in. I creep to my bedroom door and turn the handle. But I can't push it open.

I try to hold on, but soon I have to go ahead and squat in the corner. I hope Daddy won't be mad at me again.

'Kids, breakfast,' calls Kim up the stairs.

I hear the other kids running towards the kitchen, and I try the door again. It won't budge.

When I hear someone come up to use the bathroom I knock on my door. 'I'm stuck,' I shout. 'The door's gotten jammed.'

Heavy footsteps come nearer. It must be Daddy.

'Daddy, I can't get the door open.'

'Shut up, you little fucker,' he says, and walks away.

I pick up my teddy and play a little game with him, so I don't have to think about being hungry and thirsty. I make believe that Teddy is going to school and I'm his teacher. I don't go to school yet, but I know what it's like from the TV and what Mommy's told me.

Somebody's coming at last. There's a scraping at the door, like when a key is turned in a lock, and Kim comes into the room, with a dish in her hand. 'Oh, my God!' she yells. 'What a stink. You little bastard.'

She means when I had to go to the bathroom in the corner. She's right; it's smells horrible.

'I'm sorry, Kim-Mommy.'

She turns the dish she brought upside down and squashes the Coco-pops under her foot.

'I'm really hungry, Kim. Can I come downstairs and have something to eat?'

She glares at me and goes out again, and there's that scraping noise again. I'm sure she's locking me in.

'Please don't make me stay in here,' I shout. 'I promise to be good.'

There's no reply, and the house is quiet all day. I have to go to the bathroom in the corner again. I'm going to tell Mommy when I see her next weekend.

'He's burning up,' says Kim.

'He'll be okay,' says Daddy.

'How do you feel, Max?'

'Sore head,' I say.

'Did you hit him, Scott?'

'No, I didn't. Not really.'

'Well, what do you think's wrong with him?'

Daddy shrugs.

'I don't feel good,' I say quietly.

'Lock him in his room again.'

'No, please don't lock me in.'

'If you're sick we don't want the other kids catching it,' says Kim. 'Go upstairs and I'll bring you a drink.'

'Please, Kim-Mommy.'

'Do as you're told,' says Daddy.

The next day, I'm itching everywhere.

'What the hell?' says Kim. 'You've got blood on the sheets.'

'I'm sorry. I scratched myself.'

'You'd better stop that!' She checks my face and my back. 'Spots,' she says. 'You've got chickenpox. You'll have to stay in here until the spots have gone.'

This time I don't mind too much. I'm tired and I just feel like staying in bed. I wish Kim would bring me something to drink though.

When she does come up, she tells me something bad. 'No visit with your mom this weekend.'

I screw my face up and start to cry.

She slaps me. 'Stop that. It doesn't matter anyway. She never wanted you.'

'Never wanted me for what, Kim?'

'To be born, dummy. She wishes you'd never been born. And so does your dad. And me.'

'But Mommy loves me. And doesn't Daddy love me anymore?'

Kim laughs. 'No one loves you, Max. No one.'

'I want to see Mommy. Why can't I see her?'

'Because you've got chickenpox. You're not fit to see other people.'

'Please can I speak to Mommy on the phone?'

'We'll see.'

'Hello, little man. How are you feeling?'

'Sad, Mommy. Really sad. They say I can't see you.'

'I'm sorry, sweetheart. It's because you're sick, and you can make other people sick while you've got those spots.'

'They itch so much, Mommy.'

'I know, baby. But they'll soon go and then you can come see us and give us all a big hug.'

'When?'

'When you're better, Max.'

'I think I'm starting to feel better now, Mommy.'

She chuckles. 'Oh, sweetheart. I know you want to be. And I want you to be, but you're not. Not yet.'

'When will I be?'

'Soon, baby, soon. Then I'll see you again.'

'You're still my mommy, right?'

'Of course, sweetheart. And I'll always love you.'

'But Kim said you don't love …'

Kim snatches the phone away.

I can still hear Mommy's voice. 'What was he saying, Kim?'

'Oh, nothing. It's the fever; he keeps saying stupid things.'

'Let me talk to him again, Kim.'

'I'd better put him back to bed, Sara. He's looking tired.'

'Oh, okay. I'll ring tomorrow then. See how he is.'

'No, you leave it. I'll ring you if there's any change. Rest is all he needs at the moment.'

'And you're giving him plenty to drink?'

'Of course. I think we know how to take care of him, Sara.'

'I know. I'm sorry. I'll call tomorrow then.'

'No, we'll ring *you* when there's something to tell you.'

'Please ring me soon, Kim.'

'Better go, hon. Take care.'

'Say night-night to Max for me.'

'I'm better now, aren't I, Daddy? So can I come out now?'

'What do you think, Kim?'

'I guess. But I don't want any trouble from you, Max. You got that?'

'Yes, Kim-Mommy.'

'We're going trick-or-treating tonight, so you'd better behave yourself.'

I love Halloween. 'I will. I promise.' My mouth waters as I think of all the sweets we'll get.

'You didn't make him a costume, did you, Kim?' says Daddy.

'You're joking, aren't you? I've had my hands full making costumes for the rest of the kids. He can do without.'

'And no sweets for you, Max. Not after you've been ill.'

'But I'm so hungry, Daddy.'

He thumps me. 'Did you hear me?'

'Yes, Daddy. I'm sorry.'

The street is alive with witches and ghosts and fairies as I tag along behind my half-brothers and sisters. I haven't got a pumpkin bucket like they have, but I've managed to sneak some candy into my pockets. Daddy doesn't need to know.

'There you go, son.' The lady bends down and pats my shoulder. 'I bet you like milk duds.'

'They're my favourite,' I tell her.

'Well, you'd better have a few more.'

'Thank you.'

'Where's your costume, sonny?'

'I don't know. I didn't get one.'

'Max!' yells Kim. 'Stop bothering that lady.'

'He's no bother at all.'

'Come on, Max. You need to keep up.' She stops me on the corner. 'What did she give you?'

'Nothing, Kim-Mommy.'

'Hold out your hand.'

'I'm sorry.'

'Didn't we tell you not to take any sweets?'

'But I'm so hungry all the time.'

'Wait till I tell your Daddy.'

'Please don't tell him.'

She laughs. 'Right, line up, kids. I need a photo of all of you for my socials. Stand a little to the right, Max. You're spoiling the picture.'

When they get ahead of me again, I slip my hand into my pocket and eat a few sweets. But later I'm sick and Daddy beats me and sends me to my room. And I have to stay there.

'What are you doing, Kim-Mommy?'

'No more toys for you, boy,' and she starts to march out of my room with an armful of teddies and action figures.

'No! Please don't take them. I need my toys.'

'Well, you should have thought of that before you shit everywhere.'

'But I'm locked in. I can't get out to go to the bathroom.' I grab my picture book. 'Please don't take this.'

'Shut up,' she says. 'I can't stand the sound of your voice or the look of you.'

'When am I going to get out of here, Kim? I promise to be good.'

'You can stay in here forever for all I care.'

'If you let me out, I'll be so quiet. You won't even know I'm there. I know Daddy works hard and needs to rest when he's home.'

'Just shut up! You're getting on my nerves again.'

'I'm sorry, Kim. But how much longer? And what about Mommy? When am I going to see her?'

She stalks out. And I scream and cry into my pillow.

I think a whole week has passed before Daddy comes up to see me. I'm so glad I rush towards him and hug his legs.

'Get off, Max,' he says.

'I've missed you, Daddy. When will you let me out?' I've been locked in here for such a long time now, and every day when it gets light I hope that'll be the day they let me out.

'Kim doesn't give me enough to eat or drink and now she's taken my toys.'

He pushes me away. 'Because I told her to.'

What? My Daddy is doing this to me too?

'No, Daddy,' I say. 'Not you.'

He strides over to the window, pulls down the shutters, and starts hammering.

'What are you doing, Daddy?'

He doesn't answer me. But when he leaves my room again, it's completely dark, and I feel so afraid.

I lie on my bed for a long time. It's smelly and wet because I can't seem to wait to get to the corner and go to the bathroom. It happens in my sleep too.

I try and try to think what I can do to make Daddy love me again. If I knew what I did wrong, I could say "Sorry" and make sure I never do it again. Is it because I called Mommy's boyfriend "Daddy" that one time? Or because I took the Halloween sweets from that lady?

The darkness goes on and on and on.

Sometimes I throw myself around the room and scream. If they hear me they come up and I run to the corner or hide under the bed, but they drag me out and beat me.

If I ask for more to eat or drink, they give me less. Or push my face into the dish. They tell me I stink and don't deserve to be amongst normal people and be part of the family.

When I hear someone coming, and I can tell it's not Kim or Daddy, I tap on my door. But I'm too scared to tap loud enough, so they never hear me. I lean my back against the door and slide down to the floor and cry and cry. I'm so hungry. So thirsty. I turn and scratch at the door and my long nails bend backwards.

Please help me.

There's a monster living behind the window shutters. I hear it growling sometimes and see the shutter move. If it comes out it will hurt me even worse than Daddy and Kim.

I can't move around much anymore. I'm so hungry and weak. My legs can't hold me, so I sometimes crawl along the floor, although it hurts so much as I drag myself across the carpet. Daddy only comes here to beat me now, because of the mess I make.

I touch my skin, and my fingers go straight to the bone. There's nothing in between.

I keep trying to get my arms and legs moving; but I have no energy. I'll need to be strong and ready for when they take me out and let me go to school.

I'm so hungry. Please let me have something to eat.

My tummy is swelling and growing even though it's empty. I suck on a corner of the sheet which doesn't have quite so much poo on it. I try to gnaw on it, but the few threads I swallow get stuck in my throat.

The last time they came into the room to beat me, I begged them to let me out. Or at least take the tape off the window. I knew they wouldn't listen, but I'm so desperate I just begged for everything that I can't have anymore. My crying and screaming makes no difference. Nothing makes a difference at all.

They took the sheet away, and the pillow. I haven't worn clothes since they first locked me in here.

Hot or cold, winter or summer, it's just me on the bed. Lying here. I'm covered in my own mess. Under me, over me, all around me. In my hair, in my eyes, in my nose. Everywhere. A sob rises in my throat, and I howl for Mommy.

When they come in and hurt me, I can't try to hide anymore. I just have to lie here while the blows fall and my skin breaks and bleeds and I want to die from the pain.

I've made myself a new friend and his name is Mikey. Mikey gets enough to eat and drink and he can still move around. We play games together, like 'I Went To Market'. He's much better at it than I am, because I don't think so good. I can usually only remember three things. Now that I can't speak anymore it's really good that Mikey always knows what I'd like to say.

The other great thing about Mikey is that when Kim or Daddy come up to hurt me, Mikey hides me under the bed, and he takes the beating instead of me. He's so brave, and when the monster comes out from behind the window shutters, Mikey stands in front of him and doesn't let him get me.

I haven't been able to move for a long, long time. Nor speak, nor swallow. Sometimes when I breathe, the poo around me falls into my mouth and nose, and I can't cough it out again. There are no tears anymore.

Someone came to my room before; yesterday, last week, last month? I don't know. They told me they were going to throw a party for memorial day, and I'd better not make a sound. Just to be sure, they thumped my head and it bounced off the mattress and dropped back into the poo.

They told me they were leaving a meal for me and pushed a plate under the bed.

'It's fries and chicken,' they said. 'Get down on the floor and eat.'

Then they slammed the door.

If I could move, perhaps I could eat. But I can't move. Not my arm, not my leg. My fingers, just a little.

I can hear talking and laughing. I think the party must be out in the yard. I can't remember the yard. Is it big, small? Is there a slide or a swing? It might be summer. I don't know when memorial day is. But it must be today.

That's my little sister; squealing. She does that when they spray the hose around the yard and the kids run under it. If I could go under the hose I could get clean and I could take a drink.

I've said my prayers so many times. But I don't think I'm going to get out of here. This is my life now, and always.

I don't dream of escape anymore. I know it's impossible. Instead, I dream of letting go; of drifting gently away to heaven. I've had that dream so many times. That's my escape; dreaming, and finally letting go.

Mommy, I miss you. I know you'll have tried to find me, because you love me. I wish I hadn't said that to Daddy. Do you remember, Mommy, when I called your boyfriend "Daddy" and my real Daddy didn't like it? That's when it all started. If I hadn't said that, things would be different. Daddy would still love me, and Kim wouldn't hate me. I wish I could take back what I said. Aren't we supposed to forgive people when they make mistakes? I was only three or four. I don't know how old I am now.

'What the fuck? Scott come up here! Hurry up.'

'What's the little shit-bag done now?'

'I can't wake him.'

'Move over. I'll wake him. Max!'

'See? Nothing. And he's cold.'

'He's always cold, Kim. Come on, Max, wake up.'

'It's no use. He's gone. Oh God, Scott. He's dead.'

'He can't be! Max! Max!'

'Oh God, oh God, oh God.'

'What the hell are we going to do, Kim?'

'You beat him, didn't you? When you last came up here, the day before the party.'

'It was nothing. I hardly touched him. Did you feed him like I said?'

'I tried. But you know what he's like. Refused to eat.'

Scott suddenly looks around the room as if seeing it for the first time. 'He couldn't eat, Kim. How on earth could he eat?' He starts to shiver, as realisation begins to dawn. 'A starving person can't eat. Oh God, Kim, what on earth have we done?'

'We tried our best with him.'

'Did we?' He looks at the boarded window, the empty room. 'Oh dear God.'

'Scott, come on! He was such a bad kid.'

'He wasn't a bad kid.' He puts his head in his hands. 'We did it to him.'

She punches his shoulder. 'No, listen to me. He was disobedient. Look at the mess he's made in this room.'

'We didn't let him use the bathroom.'

'Only after he messed it up. What's the matter with you?'

'Kim, look at him. Are you blind? What have we done to you, son?'

'Pull yourself together, Scott.'

'Aren't you upset?'

'Of course I am. But we need to think what to do.'

'I can't think. I have to get out of here. Clear my head.'

She follows him out of the room, and I stop trying to move my finger to show I'm still alive.

The next thing I hear is a noise at the door.

'What's that almighty stink?'

'This is where they told us to come.'

'Three locks on the door. Oh God, that smell.'

It's someone new. Please help me. I'm here, on the bed. But I can't hang on, and as they burst through the door, I breathe out slowly, one last time.

An Overview of Maxwell's Case

Maxwell Schollenberger
8 December 2007 – 26 May 2020
aged 12 years & 5 months
Pennsylvania, USA

Reading any information on Max's story, the image we are left with is that the emaciated boy was caked in faeces from head to toe, in a room where every surface was similarly covered. And that he'd been in this condition 24 hours a day, 7 days a week, 12 months a year, for at least two years, and perhaps much longer. Yes, years.

It's inhuman. And yet, human beings do this, or allow this to happen.

On 26 May 2020, Kimberly Maurer opened the three locks on the bedroom door of her 12 year old stepson, Max. After subjecting the little boy to years of abuse and neglect, was she surprised to find that he had given up his fight for life?

Whatever the case, after discovering Max's body, she and her fiancé, the little boy's father, left the home, going their separate ways. Scott Schollenberger grabbed his gun and made for the next county, from where he called the police. When they reached him, officers were given the impression that he had intended to take his own life. "I was gonna join him," he told them. "I don't want to be alive."

Maurer also left the home, returning later to sit on a neighbour's porch and tell her: "Max is dead". It was the neighbour, Rhonnda Bentz, who called 911.

When police entered the home at South White Oak Street in Annville Township later that day, Officers Todd Hirsch and Jason Cleck recoiled at the stench of faecal matter that hit them as they reached the stairs leading to the upper floor. These were sights and smells they will never forget.

In one of the bedrooms, they found the naked corpse of an emaciated 12 year old boy. The only furniture in the room was the bed on which the boy was lying. There were no clothes, toys, games, tv, or books. Nothing. As they looked around the dark, faeces-ridden room, they spotted something under the bed. It was a meal of fries and chicken.

Maurer is said to have given the food to the starving boy the night before he died. But Max could not have eaten anything by this point – his empty, swollen stomach was atrophied to the extent of making digestion impossible.

Maxwell Thomas Schollenberger was born on 8 December 2007 to Sara Coon and Scott Schollenberger. When the relationship broke down, custody was awarded to his father, who lived with his girlfriend Kimberly Maurer, along with another five children; two of Scott's older children, and three that the pair had together.

According to his mother, Sara, Maxwell Schollenberger was happy, outgoing, and the image of his father, with his blond hair, blue eyes and fair skin.

Whilst Max was being starved and beaten, locked in a lightless bedroom with the windows taped up, his half-siblings seemed to be well-adjusted and healthy; enjoying a normal childhood. Their bedrooms were filled with toys and clothes, along with a flatscreen television to watch their favourite shows. With a kitchen replete with food and snacks, such as Poptarts, ice cream and candy, this was not a home that stinted on treats for the other children.

In a refrigerator filled with food, there was also beer left over from a Memorial Day party that the family had held. Max would have heard the celebration from his locked prison.

Max's siblings went to school, played games, and took part in sports. Max had none of this. He never attended school. His siblings must have felt confused about Max being treated differently; knowing that their parents kept him in his room, and that when Scott and Kim entered that room, they would hear Max scream and cry.

Maurer claimed on social media that she took Max along on trips, such as to the beach, and made him a Halloween costume. But of 10,000 photos on her phone of the other children, there is just one of Max, on Halloween 2017, standing three feet away from his half-siblings, who are dressed up and posing for the camera. Max has no costume and is clearly upset. Maurer joked on social media that she couldn't post it publicly. (Presumably due to Max's bruising.)

A news release from Lebanon County District Attorney's office describes Max's room:

"The door and its frame had not one, but three, metal hooks ... to lock the child in his bedroom. Claw marks appeared in the victim's sheets. Max Schollenberger's bedroom was entirely devoid of light and furniture, aside from the bed wherein he died."

In addition, the window blinds were taped down, and shutters were nailed shut. Max was unable to see out, and crucially, no one from the outside could see in.

Allegedly, there were also cameras around the home, in case Max was to break out of his prison.

Max died from multiple blunt force head trauma complicated by prolonged starvation, and malnutrition. Testifying in court, Dr Michael Johnson said that, shortly before he died, Maxwell had suffered a fracture to his orbital (eye socket) that would have been caused by significant force.

Max weighed 47.5 pounds (the average weight of a boy his age being 89 pounds) and measured 50 inches tall at the time of death.

Three days after Max's body was found, the scene of his torture was cleaned up, and turned into a playroom for the other children.

Three months passed before Scott Schollenberger and Kimberly Maurer were arrested, in September 2020, and charged with Max's murder.

During that time, with Sara Coon unaware of the details of the long-term abuse her son had been made to endure, Scott Schollenberger began messaging Sara on Facebook, leading to having long phone conversations with her, claiming he had nothing to do with their son's death. He seemed to be seeking forgiveness from Sara, and blaming Maurer, saying that she used to get angry with Max. Sara asked why he didn't contact her and offer her custody of her son if he was in danger.

During a pre-trial hearing, Scott pleaded guilty to criminal homicide, endangering the welfare of children, and criminal conspiracy to endanger the welfare of children, and was sentenced to life in prison without the possibility of parole.

The same charges were made against Maurer, and she chose to stand trial, thus exposing the details of Max's suffering.

The jurors were shown photos of Max as he had been found; his arms and legs wasted almost to the bone, his distended stomach that made it impossible for him to

JESSICA JACKSON

process food, the injuries from blunt force trauma to his head and body, a fractured eye socket.

Maurer's attorney, Andrew Race, alleged that Scott Schollenberger controlled the family "with an iron fist" and abused his fiancée, and that she was not allowed to make decisions about Max's care or treatment, being told, "You're just the girlfriend".

Shifting the blame onto Scott, Maurer described herself as a coward and a failure for not taking care of Max. Her attorneys argued that Scott Schollenberger was the orchestrator of his son's abuse and death.

"I thought I was doing everything I could to help Max," Maurer read from a statement.

But evidence showed that Maurer had been posting messages on social media for around nine years, mocking and belittling her stepson, saying how worthless he was and what a joy the other children were: "Maybe I should start taking pictures to prove I feed the asshole." There wasn't a single pleasant comment. "Nothing loving, nothing sweet, ever directed by her about Maxwell," said the prosecuting attorney.

Called as a witness, her fiancé said he was not aware of the messages and now that he was, he realised why Max was "doing what he was doing that I didn't see until now."

It would seem that both 'caregivers' were terrorising the little boy.

Scott Schollenberger was said to have been working 70-80 hours per week prior to the coronavirus pandemic, and alleged that after losing his job in 2020, and struggling to apply for welfare benefits, he was under great stress.

"I didn't know what to do," he testified. "But I should have done more for him."

Along with many/most other perpetrators of child abuse murder, Scott Schollenberger held Max responsible for his punishments, saying that his son didn't get along with Kim or the other children, and had bathroom accidents around the home.

"I tried to provide a better house for him, and he did nothing but destroy my second floor," Schollenberger had said in his interview with detectives, which was then played in court. He added: "The fact of the matter was I didn't check on him enough, and I wasn't there enough. That is the facts."

Both these 'caregivers' overlook one important point. IF, and I don't believe it for a second, a child is so out of control that they are randomly defecating all over the house, whatever 'punishment' is deemed necessary, eliminating the chid's access to light, human contact, and visits to his mother, are not the answers.

Bentz, the neighbour who called 911 after Max died, said she had occasionally helped Maurer financially, including buying Christmas presents for the children. "But," said Bentz. "Why couldn't she ask for help with Max? That is the question that will haunt me for the rest of my life."

Sentencing Maurer to life in prison without parole for first degree murder, with an additional 10 to 20 years for child welfare endangerment, Judge Bradford Charles said: "I have always been raised to believe there is no such thing as an unforgivable sin. But this is as close as it gets."

Lebanon County District Attorney Pier Hess Graf gave a press conference following Kimberly Maurer's sentencing. With reference to Maurer's texts and videos,

Max's stepmother complained that he was "conduct defiant" and was urinating and defecating in the home.

Maurer had claimed that she could see no way out. But Graf confirmed that the investigating officer had not witnessed Maurer shedding a tear, nor once saying that she loved Max, at any point during questioning. Graf reported that even when most of the court was weeping when viewing photos of Max's body, Maurer gave no reaction.

Describing Maurer's role in Maxwell's death as murder rather than neglect, Graf added, "It was not negligence. It was a matter of how many more days. He lay there in that stench and suffering until he died. There is no logical explanation for it. She spent so much time typing hate and vitriol when she only needed to type three numbers: 9-1-1."

DA Graf echoes what most of us feel in these horrific cases: "I think we have as good of an outcome as you can get. It's not justice. There's not justice in this. There's no bringing this child back. There's no undoing what occurred."

Rest Safely in Peace, Max

The Non-Custodial Parent

On occasion, two birth parents abuse their child to death, but most cases are of children whose parents have separated, and a step-parent has entered the scene.

When two adults find living together unbearable, and there is arguing and tension in the home, separation may be the best solution, and if there is continued close involvement of both parents, the outcome for the children can be better than if their parents had remained together.

Even when the separation is extremely amicable however, it can affect the well-being of the children to varying degrees; from feeling they are to blame for the break-up, through to being unloved and abused by a new partner.

But if one parent participates little or not at all, whether voluntarily, or because the parent who has custody shuts them out of their lives, the outcome for the children is worsened. And sometimes, the child may be tossed around on the tide of their birth parents' bitterness and their step-parents' indifference or hatred.

The interview that Maxwell's mother, Sara Coon, gave for Suffer The Little Children – which you can find online – indicates that she was a caring parent who fell on hard times and was then shut out by her former boyfriend. I don't imagine that her story is untypical.

The daughter of military parents, Sara moved around a great deal as a child, living in various locations. Then her mother died when Sara was just 17. This may have left the young woman with a feeling of instability.

Moving to Lebanon to be closer to family, she met the tall, attractive Scott Schollenberger when they both worked in the kitchens at Ruby Tuesday. After a whirlwind romance, she found that she was pregnant with Max. Her boyfriend already had a daughter and son. When Sara discovered that Scott was being unfaithful, she ended the relationship, and she moved in with a relative when Max was two years old.

Hearing a rumour that Sara was being irresponsible regarding her son's care, Scott Schollenberger walked into the house one day and took the boy away with him. Max was later placed into his father's full custody.

Sara's life unravelled. Losing her her job, she started self-harming and felt like ending it all, but became determined to pick herself up again. Finding a place in a women's shelter in Lebanon, she became pregnant with another son.

By the time Max was three years old, both parents had new partners.

Getting back on her feet, Sara Coon was spending time with Max, had a job, a car and, having a good relationship with Scott and Kim, she spent Thanksgiving with them. It appeared that they would each be able to enjoy time with their son.

Although Schollenberger seemed to be narcissistic and self-centred, Sara felt he was devoted to his children, and an excellent father. She also believed that Kim Maurer was taking good care of her son.

Whilst Sara was hurt that her little boy referred to Kimberly Maurer as 'Kim-Mommy', she accepted it as something that made her son feel more stable and happy in that home. Scott Schollenberger, however, was furious when, returning from a visit with Sara, Max called Sara's boyfriend 'Dad'.

Scott Schollenberger called Sara Coon in a rage.

After this incident, Sara felt she had to cancel the next scheduled contact two weeks later as Max had chickenpox, and she had a new baby. This must have infuriated Scott further, as from that moment, he ended all contact between Sara and Max.

Bad luck followed Sara. Both she and her boyfriend lost their jobs, and they couldn't pay the rent. Moving out of state to live with friends, Sara could pay support for Max only intermittently, and felt she would be arrested if she moved back to Lebanon.

Hoping to be reunited with Max when he grew older, Sara then had to be satisfied with watching her son grow up via photos on social media. With Scott keeping in touch with her, and pictures of Max on vacation with his family, she felt reassured that he was happy and well cared for.

But eventually, Scott blocked her and wouldn't answer her calls. She started emailing him, but that eventually stopped too. And the snapshots of her son's life dried up. It was many years later before she discovered the reason why.

Readers of my books know that I'm not judgemental about family (or others) who loved and tried to protect the murdered child. Some people, however, vent their fury at an absent parent who didn't remain closely involved in their child's life. I can completely understand that, as bringing a child into the world is a shared responsibility, which doesn't end with separation or divorce.

In an ideal world, even when pushed out by the custodial parent, unless the non-custodial parent has been abusing the child, all efforts should be made to ensure they remain a stable, loving, and protective   presence in their children's lives. When they are not, as happened in Max's case, the child loses a powerful advocate for their safety and well-being.

Falling Star

'Hey, Frankie. It's me, Jodie.'

'Hi, Jodie. How's it going?'

'Good, really good. But you've been busy.'

The younger girl laughs. 'Yeah, a bit.'

I peek into the pram. 'Oh, she's absolutely gorgeous.'

Frankie grins. 'She can be a real devil at times.'

'I don't believe you. She's like a little button.' I hesitate. I long to hold her, but since my miscarriage I've lost my confidence, and I get nervous in case I make babies cry.

Frankie makes the decision for me. 'You can hold her if you like.'

I pick her up gingerly, and it soon feels good to have the tiny girl in my arms. 'She's so cute, Frankie. You still with the same lad?'

'Oh yeah.' She laughs. 'For now.'

I lift the baby up towards my nose. 'Mmm, that smell. What have you called her?'

'Star,' she says proudly.

'Gorgeous name. You look really happy, hun.'

'I'm hoping to get my own flat soon and have some independence.'

'Oh great. I'm glad things are working out for you.'

'I'm not gonna lie; it was hard after you moved away. You protected me from those bullies when we were kids.'

'They were pretty nasty, weren't they?'

'I–I've always wanted to thank you for what you did.'

'Aww, no probs, babes. I did worry about you after I left though.'

'But you're back now?'

'I'm working round here. Training to be a social worker.'

'No way! You always were a brain box. Wow, that's amazing.'

'It's hard work, but I love it. In fact, I'm hoping to work with kids when I qualify.'

'You'll be good at that. I mean it, Jodie. You'll stick up for kids getting hurt. Kids like me.'

'You were too soft, Frankie. You never stood up for yourself.'

'I know. But now I've got Star, I'd stand up to anyone to protect her.'

'That's what I like to hear. Look, I'd better go, but it's been great to see you again.' I hand the little bundle back to her mother.

'You too, Jodie. Bye.'

'Stay safe, honey.' I watch her pushing the pram along the street. She must have only just turned 18, but it really suits her.

'I'm telling you, Jodie, she's definitely got her eye on you.'

'Who? I haven't noticed anyone.'

'The one in the green top. Been watching you all night. I've seen her before. She's a bouncer in one of the pubs.'

I turn slightly, trying not to look too obvious. Heck, that top's a really bright green. 'She looks nice enough, but I don't think I'm ready yet, Desti.'

'Ready? For what? She'll only want to buy you a drink or have a dance.'

'I don't know. I'm just not comfortable in here yet.'

'You'll soon get used to it. Have another shot and relax. Then we'll have a dance. Okay?'

'Okay. But I might go home soon.'

'Two Kamikazes please, Alison.'

'Coming up.' As Alison puts the drinks on the bar, she looks me straight in the eye. 'Listen, sister. There's nothing to be scared of. Everyone in here is just like you. Some are even as nervous as you are. Take your time and enjoy yourself.'

'Do I look so terrified?'

'Like a rabbit in the headlights. Now get that down you and get on that dance-floor.'

Desti grabs my arms as 'Rain On Me' pulses around the room.

Green-top-girl is on me in a heartbeat. 'Hey, darling.'

'Oh yeah, hi,' I shout above the music. She's actually quite pretty.

'Not seen you here before. First time out?'

'Yeah, that's right.'

'You'll be fine. They're a nice crowd in here.'

'Seem to be. Loving the music.'

'Ah, you new girls. It's all about the music.' She arches her eyebrows. 'Until it becomes all about the girls.'

'Well, that too. I mean ...'

'Don't worry, hun. And if you have any trouble, give me a shout. I'm Savannah.'

'Jodie.'

'I know,' she says, with a wink.

A wink? A girl is winking at me? I thought that went out in the nineties along with wolf whistles from builders.

'Anyway, good to meet you, darling. See you around.' And she grabs the waist of a pale, dark haired girl who's been waiting for her.

'Thought you'd clicked then,' laughs Desti.

'Not exactly. Still, it was nice to flirt with a girl for the very first time.'

'Hey, don't I count for anything?'

I nudge my friend's arm. 'No, not really.'

Desti and me become regulars at the club, and although I still don't really know what I want, or who I want, we always have a great time. Bright lights, dancing, drinking and laughing are a good way to forget all the troubled families I have to deal with at work.

My first time at The Queer Christmas Party is heavenly.

As I flop back down on my seat, draped in tinsel, a girl appears at my side.

'I'm sorry, I'm just too tired,' I say, then look up. 'Frankie! What are you doing here?' As soon as I've said it I feel terrible. Hell, she has as much right to be here as anyone.

'I'm with my girlfriend,' she says quietly. So quietly I can hardly hear her above the music. 'This is Savannah.'

'Oh, wow! Hi, Savannah. We've met before. How's things?'

'Have we?' says Savannah.

I'm glad the house lights are down so they can't see my blush. 'Well, yeah. A few months ago. Right here, in fact.'

She shrugs. 'You two certainly seem to know each other.'

'When we were kids,' says Frankie. 'Jodie was like a big sister to me.'

'Oh, was she now?' says Savannah.

'Hey, Frankie, how's Star? Still as cute as a button?'

'Star's fine,' says Savannah. 'Come on, Frankie. I need another drink.'

'That was weird,' says Desti. 'To be honest, your friend Frankie looked as if she didn't dare put a foot wrong. You know what I'm saying?'

'I do. I hope she's okay.'

'That Savannah can be a bit of a nutter, you know. I've heard some stuff about her. Hey, come on, it's a party. Let's dance!'

When the referral lands on my supervisor's desk a few weeks later, I hesitate for a moment.

'Little girl, eight months old. Lesbian couple.'

I can sense the disapproval, and I wince. 'What's the deal?'

'Unexplained injuries. Possibly non-accidental. Photos are in here somewhere.'

I spot the name on the file, and take a deep breath. 'I know the family. Only vaguely, but I do know them.'

'You can't be on the case then, Jodie.'

'I know. I just hope they're okay. The baby and the mum.'

'Let's hope so. Right, I'll assign you to a different case.'

I start to wish I hadn't spoken up.

'You understand, don't you, Jodie?'

'Yeah, of course. Can you keep me informed though?'

She touches my arm. 'That should be okay.'

'Frankie! Hey, Frankie!'

'Oh, hey Jodie.'

'Great to see you. How's things?'

She shrugs.

'And how's this one?' I reach forward to say "hi" to Star, but she shrinks back. I think of the referral. 'She okay, Frankie?'

'She's fine.'

I crouch down, but the little girl still seems unsure of me. 'That a cut above her eye?'

'Yeah, you know kids. Now she's toddling about, she falls all the time.'

'Aww, sweetheart, I'm not going to hurt you.'

'She's just a bit nervous around new people.'

I stroke Star's arm and she gives me a shy smile. 'I bet you like chocolate, do you, baby?'

She glances up at Frankie, then nods.

I fumble in my pocket where I've got two packets of chocolate buttons. I'm on my way to see my nephews and never go empty handed. They'll have to share today though.

Star's beautiful big eyes seem to grow wider as I hand her the sweets.

'No,' says Frankie, grabbing them from her. 'She's been naughty and isn't allowed sweets for a while.'

'Aww, I'm sorry. Hey, Star, your mummy will keep them for you for later, okay?'

Star nods, then stretches out her hand and grabs my fingers.

'Oh, baby. You're so precious.'

'We should be going,' says Frankie.

'Just one more minute. I think she's talking to me.'

In the tiniest voice, Star has started to sing her version of 'Twinkle Twinkle Little Star.'

It's so beautiful I want to cry. But I join in instead. When we get to the end I hold out my arms, and not afraid anymore she comes in for a cuddle.

'Can I pick her up, Frankie?'

I sense her hesitation. 'Please.' Although I've played plenty of rough and tumble games with my nephews since the miscarriage, Star's the only child I've actually held in my arms, and I ache to do it again. Tentatively, I lift her up and hold her close, hoping Frankie won't see my tears. 'You're so lucky, Frankie.'

'Yeah, maybe.'

'And I bet everybody loves you to pieces.' I nuzzle into Star's neck. 'Who loves you, Star?'

'Gan-pa. Gan-ma. A-ty …'

'Aww, your grandma and grandpa and aunties; they love you, Star?' I say. 'I remember your sisters, Frankie. How are they doing?'

She shrugs. 'Okay, I suppose.'

'I bet they adore this little one. And we can't forget Mummy, can we, Star? She loves you the most.'

Star looks at Frankie, but stays silent.

'Can I take her home with me?' I smile.

'Everyone says that. Come on, Star. Savannah will be waiting for us.'

I feel her tiny body stiffen, and the warmth leaves her eyes, as I set her on her feet.

'Bye bye, Star,' I say, as I watch Frankie dragging her down the street.

Star looks back at me, and waves her tiny fingers.

The next time I see Star, she's out in Devonshire Park with Frankie and Savannah. But instead of pushing her on the swings or running around on the grass, Savannah is pulling Star along the path by her reins. Frankie turns away as I start to walk up to them.

'Hey, you two. Hey, Star.'

Star immediately holds out her arms to me and my heart melts, but Savannah jerks her backwards and she stumbles.

'How's it going?' I say.

'Who the hell are you?' says Savannah. 'Coming up to my family like you know us.'

'But I do know you, and you know me. I've met you at least twice, hun, and I know Frankie from when we were kids.'

She turns to Frankie. 'You know this person?'

Frankie shakes her head. 'I don't think so.'

'Well, that's settled then. We don't know you and we don't want to know you.'

'I don't get it, Savannah. We met at the club, about a year ago. And I've seen Frankie and Star around town.' I crouch down and Star smiles shyly. 'We're friends, aren't we, Star?'

'Like I said,' says Savannah. 'We don't know you, so fuck off.'

'Can I just give Star something to buy an ice cream?' I straighten up and dig a £2 coin out of my pocket.

'What is it you don't understand, bitch?' says Savannah, squaring up to me. 'If you say one more word, it's harassment. Got it?'

They leave me on the spot, in shock. Something is very wrong.

'Bloody hell, Jodie, you seen this?'

When lockdown started, Desti and me decided we'd stay together in my apartment to keep each other company. But we're starting to get on each other's nerves, and although I'm mostly working from home, lots of my colleagues are off sick with the virus, and I'm shattered after a really long day. We took in a rescue puppy too, and she's adorable, but such hard work.

I close my eyes and hope Desti will be quiet, and that I won't be called upon to look after Bella right now. No such luck; Desti elbows me in the ribs. 'Jodie, you have to see this. Have you sent a friend request to your old friend Frankie?'

'Uhm, yeah. I might've done. Why?'

'Watch this.' She plays a snapchat video of Savannah warning people not to contact her girlfriend if they want to keep their kneecaps.

I sigh. 'I hope Frankie's okay. Savannah calls herself a psycho, and she bloody well is one.'

'You need to steer clear, Jodie.'

'Well, I can't do much else at the moment, even if I wanted to see her.'

'Lockdown sucks,' says Desti. 'But seriously, Jodie. Please be careful.'

The next day, I FaceTime Linda, my supervisor, and ask about Star.

'Oh, I'm sorry, hun. We closed her case ages ago. It was definitely an accidental fall.'

'Definitely?'

'Yeah, don't worry. Not your case, remember?'

'Let me show you something.' I send her link to the snapchat video.

'Hmm, thanks, Jodie. She does seem a bit aggressive. But without anything further there's nothing we can do.'

'Will you visit them? Please, Linda.'

'Okay, I will. But that's where it ends. And I can't report back to you on everything.'

'As long as I know you're taking another look.'

'Try not to worry, Jodie.'

But I do worry, of course. I haven't slept well since seeing that video. Possessiveness like that can turn out to be dangerous.

I wish I knew where the rest of Frankie's family lived these days. Or Star's Daddy's family. I seem to remember that he was a decent lad.

I'm sure the social workers aren't doing enough to protect Star. So I try to make it my business to be around Frankie's flat, to see if I can spot anything.

With it being lockdown, the whole town is practically deserted, and I'll have to explain myself to the police if they spot me out and about like this. Once, I think I hear a child screaming, but it turns out to be a cat.

'Desti, I need you to do me a huge favour.'

She looks up from her iPad. 'Anything, sweetheart.'

'You might not like it.'

'Try me.'

'I can't stop thinking about Frankie's baby. I need you to ring my office and tell them you're worried they're hurting her. I know it's a lot to ask, but I can't do it. They'll know my voice.'

''Course I'll do it. Give me the address. I'll pretend I'm in the flat next door. But go out of the room. I can't do it with you listening.'

'You're a pal, thanks.'

After a few minutes, she calls me back into the lounge. 'All done. They're going to do a welfare check.'

I hug my friend. Maybe she's not too bad to live with after all.

As I grab Bella's lead from its hook, she begins her usual scooting up and down the hallway, making her funny little yodelling noise. A tiny Cavapoo, she loves her morning walks in the park before I go to work.

'We're just off, Desti. You need anything from the shop while we're out?'

No reply.

'Desti? Desti, you gone deaf?'

I put my head round the kitchen door. 'Everything okay, Desti?' I say, as I grab the piece of toast suspended in mid-air, halfway to her mouth. 'You not hungry, babes?'

Desti still doesn't move, or speak.

'You're scaring me, hun. What gives?' Then I notice she's paused the TV on the local news. The still image looks familiar. 'That's the flats where Frankie lives.'

She turns to me at last. 'There's been a death there.'

'Oh, okay. Someone you know?'

'Someone we both know, I guess.' She presses play.

'A little girl who was taken to Bradford Royal Infirmary A&E last night has been pronounced dead. Star Hobson, of Halifax Road, Keighley …'

An Overview of Star's Case

Star Alicia Hobson
21 May 2019 – 22 September 2020
aged 1 year & 4 months
West Yorkshire, England

Frankie Smith was just shy of her 18th birthday when she gave birth to a beautiful baby daughter. With her own loving family, and that of her little girl's father, welcoming the baby and giving their support, the young mother had the world at her feet.

In addition to Frankie's youth, she was generally known to be a naive young woman, with an IQ in the bottom 2%, and when the couple's relationship broke down a few months later, Frankie Smith began to struggle, and her grandparents cared for Star for three months over the winter of 2019/2020.

When Smith moved into her own flat in early 2020, she took her baby daughter into her home, with her family hoping that the fresh start would benefit them both, whilst they stayed alert for signs of trouble.

They found it in Smith's new partner, Savannah Brockhill.

Brockhill, an amateur boxer, and bouncer (door security) at The Sun pub in nearby Bradford, dominated the subservient Smith, and began to isolate her from friends and family, warning that social media friend requests to her lover would be met with violence.

Just before the UK coronavirus lockdown in March 2020, Brockhill suspected that Smith might be seeing someone else, and she warned Smith's sister via video that she was 'psycho' and that she would 'stab someone tonight'.

Smith's family and friends were right to take such threats seriously. Brockhill was violent towards her younger lover, and had also told a friend that she felt like driving them both off a cliff. Sadly, when Brockhill and Smith had arguments within their volatile relationship, they took out their anger on the defenceless child. Once the argument was over, it might be forgotten by the adults, but Star was emotionally and physically scarred.

In addition, perhaps influenced by Brockhill, Smith began to view Star's behaviour – that of a normal toddler exploring her world and learning about her environment –

as wilfully 'naughty', enabling Smith to justify punishing her baby daughter.

Smith's family lived in the affluent village of Baildon, and although her parents had separated, she maintained good relationships with her family, and when she was younger, she and her mother had lived next door to her grandparents, with whom she developed a strong bond.

Prior to becoming pregnant with Star, Frankie Smith used to socialise in the local pubs, often with her mum, who was still a young woman herself. Yvonne Spendley described Frankie as: "the girl who never grew up", who played with dolls into her late teens, left school with no qualifications, didn't really have any ambitions, and had never had a job. She felt that her daughter was innocent and vulnerable.

Her words tie in with a report by a police psychiatrist, who later reported that Smith was "abnormally compliant and abnormally prone to going along with what an authority figure is telling her to do".

When signs of abuse to Frankie's baby were becoming apparent, Star's wider family were desperate to protect her, and began reporting their concerns to social services and the police. As a result, Smith and Brockhill did all they could to shut them out of Star's life. Seeing photos online that concerned them further, relatives continued to call. Cases were opened and closed a number of times, when after brief investigations the authorities believed the couple when they claimed that Star's injuries were caused by her falling against a coffee table, playing with a puppy, or falling down the stairs. They also noted that the reports may have been "malicious" due to prejudice against a gay couple, and the fact that Brockhill came from a travelling family.

When they would not act to protect the little girl, Star's great-grandmother ominously predicted to social services: "We don't want another Baby P on our hands."

As well as Smith's loving grandparents and siblings, Star's babysitter, and a friend of Frankie's mum also reported abuse to the authorities. In the latter instance, the case that was opened as a result, in June 2020, was closed on 15 September 2020, just days before Star's murder.

Frankie's family desperately tried to get her to leave Brockhill, assuring her that she could take out a restraining order against her if she was afraid, but to no avail.

Clips online show Brockhill holding an anxious and confused Star; some can see terror in the baby's eyes. Brockhill is said to have used wrestling moves to restrain her, while Smith stood by.

On another occasion, Smith is seen dragging her weakened daughter along the street by her reins, despite Star being unable to walk, due to a broken leg.

Eight days before Star's murder, Brockhill is known to have launched a three-hour assault on the tiny girl, punching her repeatedly in the stomach and face.

On the day of her murder, Star was beaten and stomped on. Her murderers searched online for what to do for shock in babies, before calling 999.

Star's death was due to catastrophic abdominal injuries. She was also found to have more than 30 other injuries, including rib fractures, two breaks in her right tibia caused by forced twisting, and a 12cm fracture on the back of her skull.

During the trial, Smith told the court that Brockhill had murdered Star while she had done nothing to prevent it.

Frankie Smith was sentenced to eight years for causing or allowing Star's death. Attorney General, Suella Braverman, said this was "unduly lenient" and the Court of Appeal increased the sentence to 12 years.

Her former partner, Savannah Brockhill, must serve at least 25 years for murder.

Star's great-grandfather, David Fawcett, remembers the happy baby who loved to dance along as he played Beatles' songs on his guitar, but after her death said: "She went to Hell before she went to Heaven."

This Youtube clip from ITV news shows Star dancing and smiling, and then her anxiety around Brockhill, and the bruises on her face: **https://www.youtube.com/watch?v=v9ccsEDFkXs**

My grateful thanks to Linda from the UK
for requesting Star's story.

Rest safely in peace, Star

Covid-19 Lockdown

When coronavirus began to spread around the world in early 2020, I was pretty nervous. For myself, my family, my friends, and for the vulnerable, such as the elderly.

But something preyed on my mind even more strongly when national "lockdowns" were imposed, severely restricting citizens' freedoms and instructing them to stay at home. What on earth was going to happen to abused children? They were now being legitimately trapped at home, and oversight was going to be minimal. I feared the increase in abuse and abused to death cases to come.

Between April 2020 and March 2021, a report by SACPA (Safeguarding and Child Protection Association) states that there was an increase of 19% in cases of death or serious harm to a child due to abuse or neglect.

The two best known UK murders around that time, are of Star Hobson and six year old Arthur Labinjo-Hughes.

Arthur's father, Thomas Hughes, moved in with his girlfriend, Emma Tustin, at the beginning of the first lockdown in March 2020, and by June, Arthur had endured weeks of unspeakable mental and physical cruelty, and was dead.

In Arthur's case, when family members alerted the authorities to the abuse, at least one of them, his caring uncle, was told he could be prosecuted under lockdown rules if he persisted in trying to visit Arthur at home. It is as hard to imagine the anguish of Daniel Hughes and other loving family members, knowing the little boy was being abused, as it is to understand the utter stupidity of leaving the child in a place of danger with no source of comfort.

We don't always know the details of what goes on behind closed doors. In Arthur's case, we have extremely distressing video evidence of his stepmother's cruelty.

Arthur is one of an increasing number of children whose torture was recorded on CCTV cameras, installed to ensure he didn't move from his 14 hour per day instruction to stand in the hallway of the family home, isolated and desperate. Emma Tustin also had over 200 recordings of Arthur's distress on her phone, where the distraught child can be heard crying: "No one loves me" and "No one is going to feed me". Arthur's father's response to one message that Tustin sent him was a horrifying and dismissive three words: "Just end him." I had not planned to tell Arthur's story in my books, but the compassion I feel while merely writing down this brief summary leads me to think I may do so.

Star's case has brought up several questions for me. There is little doubt in my mind that Frankie Smith was dominated by Savannah Brockhill and was a victim of her violence and control. Prior to meeting Brockhill, as a young single mother, Frankie had already found herself temporarily unable to care properly for Star, and her grandparents had stepped in. But I have not discovered any incidents of severe neglect or abuse before Brockhill arrived on the scene.

Those who have not experienced it may find the power of coercive control hard to understand. But it does take over the lives of many people who fall prey to a controlling, dominant partner.

In child murder, we have seen numerous cases where a partner who does not actively participate in, but does not prevent, the abuse of a child, sometimes escapes without any charges being brought against them. This is now changing. And I agree that it should, because whatever the cost to the adult, the child must come first. It's easy for us to say that no one should have children if they can't nurture and protect them, and I wish with all my heart that we could impose that. But in the meantime, we have (mostly very young) adults like Frankie Smith, not challenging her dominant partner, and soaking up beliefs around what constitutes naughty behaviour and increasingly accepting violent punishments as the norm.

If You Tell

I watch my dad being driven away and I know he's not coming back. He's been an okay dad, I guess, but he's done bad things, and we both know he's going down this time. I wish Mom was around more, but she has problems of her own. I don't have much other family. Except for my aunt and my cousins. They're pretty neat.

So I sleep out for a few nights, then show up at Aunt Shelly's door.

'Hey, Shane.' She holds out her arms and welcomes me in. 'We've all been looking forward to seeing you, son. A real man in the family.'

I glance at my step-uncle but he just smiles and reaches out his hand for me to shake. 'Good to have you here, Shane. How old are you now?'

I puff out my chest. 'Thirteen.'

'Like I said, a real man,' smiles my auntie.

'I won't stay for long, Auntie Shell. Just till I get myself sorted.'

'Sure, sure. But stay as long as you like. I heard that no-good brother of mine got himself into trouble and your mom's using again?'

'Yeah, I guess.'

'Well, you don't need to worry anymore; you're with us now. We'll soon get somewhere set up for you to sleep.'

My cousins come forward shyly. 'Hi, Shane.'

They're nice girls. Maybe we can help each other with homework and chores and maybe we'll shoot some hoops and stuff.

'Oh, wow! I never had a room like this before.'

'I told you, Shane. You're one of us now.'

My room in the basement has brand new bedding, and new school clothes laid out on the bed. I hug my auntie.

'I think it'd work out better if you started calling us Mom and Dad from now on, don't you, Shane?'

'For sure? You mean it?'

'Course we mean it, son,' says Uncle Dave. 'You're part of the family.'

'Thanks, Dad.' I hug Shelly again. 'Thanks, Mom. You're the best.'

'Right, I think it's about time you got started on your chores, Shane. That's what we do in this house.'

'Sure, Mom,' I say, excited to be pitching in. 'Just tell me where to start.'

The pretty blonde with the curls is nudging her friend.

'I want you all to make Shane welcome,' says the teacher. 'Help him out with where we keep things.'

'Yes, Ma'am,' says a brunette sitting across from me.

The teacher smiles. 'And I don't just mean the girls. You boys, too.'

A hand shoots up. 'We can take him onto the sports field at recess.'

'Good idea, Ronnie. You like sports, Shane?'

'I sure do, Ma'am. Track and soccer and a little baseball.'

'You'll fit right in, Shane –'

Another boy interrupts her. 'You could join our school teams, Shane. It's about time we won something.'

The whole class laughs. I'm going to like it here.

At recess, a few of the girls, giggling and blushing, follow us onto the field. I remember how some of the street runaways used to say I was good looking, and I realise my classmates are flirting with me. It feels good.

'Why don't you girls go back and play 'Chase' in the yard?' says one of the boys.

'We like it up here,' says Blonde-Curls. 'We can be here if we want.'

'You haven't been up here the whole year,' says Ronnie, with a shrug. 'Don't mind them, Shane. Looks like they got ants in their pants for the new boy.'

'Oh, I don't mind,' I say, winking at Blonde-Curls.

The girls run back to the yard, shrieking, and looking back to see if I'm watching.

'SHANE!'

Mom sure can shout. And it seems like I didn't do my chores as good as she wants, because I have to do them all again. My cousin Nikki kneels beside me as we scrub the kitchen floor.

'Your mom isn't quite so sweet as I thought she was,' I say.

'You got that right. But everybody thinks she's as nice as pie.'

'She's been so good to me, Nikki. I've got to do my best by her.'

'You can try,' she says. 'But sometimes there's no pleasing her.'

'Get on with it, kids,' yells Mom from the sofa.

I snigger. 'What's the betting she's eating about six Oh Henry! bars?'

'And what do you think? Is she watching a soap, or reading a magazine?' says Nikki. 'I'm going for The Young and The Restless.'

'I'll take 'magazine' then.' I shuffle to the door. The TV is playing softly. 'You win, Nikki; it's General Hospital, but it's TV, so you win.'

'Shane!'

'Yes, Mom.'

'Make me another tuna sandwich, and not so much pickle this time.'

'Where've you been, Shane?'

'Just to the bathroom, Mom. Did you want me?'

'Well, yes I do. You see, in this house, we ask permission before we use the bathroom.'

I laugh, but then see her face is serious. 'You mean it? I need to ask permission?' I'm waiting for her to laugh and tell me she's joking.

'We've got rules in this house, Shane. And I'd sure like you to abide by them.'

'But the bathroom, Mom?'

'You got a problem with that, you know what you can do. You got a problem?'

'No, no problem. I guess I didn't know about that rule. I'm sorry, Mom.'

'That's okay. But I still have to punish you, Shane. Get out in the yard.' She calls to my uncle. 'Dave, I need your help here.'

Auntie Shelly has a weird look on her face, and I'm not sure what's coming. But I don't think they'll punish me too hard. I'm wrong though.

'Take off your shirt and pants.'

I look around. None of the girls are in sight, so I pull off my clothes.

'You got the hose, Dave?'

'All ready, honey.'

'Stand right there, Shane. And remember, this is for your own good. So you learn the house rules and be a part of the family.' She nods to Uncle Dave.

'Aaghh, what the hell?' The cold water blasts my skin and I'm on the ground in an instant. 'Turn it off!'

'Stand up, Shane. And take your punishment like a man.'

I scramble to my feet, and manage to stay upright for a few seconds as my aunt instructs my uncle where to direct the hose. I soon fall to the ground again.

'Looks like you need some practice staying on your feet, son,' says my aunt. 'Hey, Nikki.' I guess my cousin must've come into view. 'Get over here and wallow with your cousin. You left your bed in a messy heap of blankets this morning.'

Nikki trudges across to join me.

'Not like that, girl. Dear Lord. Take your things off. Come on now, you know better than that.'

And my cousin has to take off her jeans and shirt and step up to the jet in just her bra and panties. Her feet soon slip from under her and we lie together in the mud, battered by the hose, until Aunt Shelly tells Dave we've had enough.

'There now. Doesn't that feel better? All that disobedience and untidiness washed clean away. Go grab a towel and then you can have hot coffee and biscuits.'

When I go down to my room later, my pillow is gone. I head back upstairs.

'Mom, did you take my pillow to wash?'

She looks up from her magazine with one of her sweet smiles. 'Now, why would I want to go and do something like that?'

'It's not on my bed, Mom. So I thought …'

'I took the pillow, Shane, so you don't forget the house rules. What sort of a mother would I be if I just expected you to remember every little thing without some kind of reminder, huh?'

'Oh. I'm sorry for making the mistake before.'

'Hey, that's okay, son. I'm just making sure you don't do it again.'

'But my pillow, Mom. How am I going to sleep?'

'I'm sure you'll manage. How about you go back down now and see how you get on? Night, Shane.'

And I have to go down to the basement, lie on my bed, and think about what on earth's happening.

'Hi, Shane.' The cute blonde girl reaches the school gates at the same time as I do. 'I'm Becky.'

'I know. I mean, I …' I feel myself blushing. *What a dork I am.* 'Hi, Becky.'

'Some of us stick around after school and talk and goof around. It'd be great if you stayed and joined us.'

'I'm not sure, Becky.' God, she's cute. 'I have to do chores when I get home.'

'I'm sure your mom wouldn't mind just one time. It's no big deal. We just drink sodas and tell jokes and stuff.'

'I live with my aunt and uncle. They've been good to me, and I don't like to let them down.'

'That's a pity. It would've been good to see you after school.'

'I'd have liked it too.' I can hardly look at her, she's so pretty.

'If you can ever make it, we meet by the old climbing bars.' She slips her hand into mine. I wish mine wasn't so big and rough.

In the next moment, she's gone; scooting away to her first class.

I think about Becky all morning. Her soft little hand. Her sweet dimples. When we're in the same class for math, I watch her leaning over the desk, working out the problem, with her tongue peeking out the side of her mouth.

She glances back and sees me looking. I'm too slow to look away and she smiles. I manage to smile back without turning bright red again. I see her scribbling a note and I know it's for me before she even passes it back to the girl in the row between us.

'Meet me at recess?'

When she looks again, I nod.

This time, I take her hand, and we go out towards the field.

It's her turn to blush. 'I'm not usually so forward,' she says. 'But all the girls like you, so I had to be the first to let you know, in case you picked someone else.'

'I liked you from the beginning,' I say. I can't resist teasing her though. 'But tell me about all the other girls liking me.'

She looks a little upset until she sees me starting to laugh.

'I don't care about them, Becky. You're beautiful.' I can't believe I'm saying this. It's the first time I've ever liked a girl. But I do like her. A lot.

There's a few other boys and girls holding hands, walking near the field, all looking for a quiet spot. We find ours and she turns to me, standing on her tiptoes. I dip my head down towards her and brush my lips against her cheek. Then we both tilt our faces and our lips touch.

I run my hand through her hair. 'You're lovely.'

All too soon, a whistle pierces the air, with the gym teacher on the end of it, telling all the kids to move it, and Becky and me run back to the main schoolyard, still holding hands.

We leap off the dirt bike and go running into the woods.

'Wow!' says Nikki. 'I *love* that.'

'Great, isn't it?' I say over my shoulder, still running.

Nikki spreads out her arms as she strides out, jumping over the tree roots. 'And I love this, too.'

When we get tired we flop down onto the ground, laughing.

'What a feeling,' says Nikki.

'It's called freedom.'

'It feels fantastic.'

We try to catch our breath, but it's hard when we're laughing so much.

Nikki picks up a pine cone, turning it over in her fingers. 'Better not tell Mom how much we're enjoying ourselves.'

'She'd soon put a stop to it,' I laugh.

But Nikki looks serious. 'She would, Shane. We can't tell her.'

'Okay. God, your mom is batshit crazy.'

Nikki shrugs. 'She *is* kind of weird.'

'Everyone does what she tells them. Man, the things she gets your dad to do.'

'And she makes us feel we did bad things, when it's nothing at all.'

'Tries to make us feel guilty. Then blame each other instead of her. Or blame ourselves.'

Nikki nods. 'I'm sorry she included you in the drenching with the hosepipe.'

'Now that wallowing is totally crazy.'

'Were you embarrassed, Shane?'

'Sure was.'

'I'm sorry.'

'Hey, it's not your fault. See, she's got us blaming ourselves.'

'Shane?'

'Yeah?'

'Are you scared of Mom?'

I pause. I'm a teenage boy. Almost a man. I shouldn't be scared of my auntie. 'Yes, I am. You never know what's gonna happen next.'

'And you can never avoid it. When she's after you, she's after you. That's it.'

'I'm gonna get away, Nikki.'

'You mean run away?'

I nod. 'I'll find somewhere to live and come back for you.'

Mom is waiting for us in the yard. The next day, the dirt bike is gone.

'I did warn you, Shane.'

'But I didn't do anything wrong.'

'And that's the trouble; you don't even realise the stuff you're doing.'

'But I need a shower, Mom. I can't go to school like this.'

'Then you should have thought of that before.'

'Please, Mom. Please. And I can't find my other set of school clothes.'

'Oh, can't you? Never mind. You can manage with one.'

'Why are you doing this, Mom?'

'Don't sass me, Shane. Remember I took you in when no one wanted you.'

I have no answer for that, because it's true. But I need to get away from this crazy woman and her crazy husband.

'I think I see her car.'

'That's just the dust blowing.'

'No, look, she's coming.'

And sure enough, a car is winding up the road and coming to a stop on the driveway.

Grandma Lara steps into the yard and holds out her arms.

We all run towards her. Boy, does she smell good.

Grandma Lara is my real dad and Aunt Shelly's stepmom, but she treats us better than kin. Presents tumble out of her bag, and she laughs as we scoop them up.

'Don't spoil them,' says Mom.

'It's a pretty sad state of affairs if I can't spoil my grandkids once in a while, Shelly.'

We've cleaned up the girls' rooms for Grandma to see, but have been warned not to let her go near the basement.

'And what about you, Shane? Where's your room?'

'Oh, you don't want to see that,' says Mom.

'No, I really do. I'd love to see where my grandson sleeps.'

'A teenage boy's cave? Oh boy, you *really* don't want to see that.'

'Come on, Shane, show me. Smelly socks and all.'

Mom shrugs. I've never seen her back down before.

Grandma retches as we go down the steps. 'What's that stink? That's not socks!'

'Oh, it's just diesel fumes.'

'I don't know how you can bear it. Oh Shane, where's your bed? And a closet for your clothes?'

I look at Mom. She took them away when I was too long sweeping the yard.

'We're onto it. You know what kids are like; he can't decide what he wants, can you, son?'

'Well, he can't sleep here. A thin mattress on a concrete floor!'

'Furniture doesn't come cheap, Lara. Neither does looking after kids. You know that.'

Grandma opens her purse and takes out her wallet. 'Get him something decent, Shelly.'

But I never get that bed, or a closet.

'Hey, Shane.'

'Hey, Becky.'

'What happened to your eye? That looks painful.'

'Nothing. It's fine. How you doing, babes?'

'Great. You wanna come to my place tonight? My folks will be out till ten.'

'I wish I could. But, you know, chores.'

'Do you still like me, Shane?'

''Course I do. It's just, I don't have the freedom some of you guys have.'

'But I've never seen you outside school. Not one time.'

'I know. I'm sorry. My aunt's been so good to me, but I have to help out a lot at home. To thank her, I guess.'

Becky squeezes my hand, and somehow I can tell she's tired of waiting for me to be a proper boyfriend.

'See you at recess?'

'Sure, Shane. See you.'

But instead she sends her friend. 'Becky says she's sorry. She had to be somewhere.'

I scuff the ground. 'Okay.'

'Look, Shane. She's never said anything; she's not a mean person. None of us are. But we can't help noticing. Like, when did you last have a shower?'

She doesn't wait for me to answer.

At lunch break, the guys scoot off to the ball field without me, and when I show up they say they already have enough players.

I put my hands in my pockets and mooch around. All the little groups of friends stare and then turn away as I approach them. Somehow I can't get the courage to go join one of them. I can tell they don't want me around.

'Right, you two,' says Mom. 'I've had enough of this.'

'Of what, Mom?'

'Don't answer me back, girl. You know what you've done.'

These are the worst times. The times that make you wrack your brains to think what sin you've committed. But never knowing. Never being able to say you're sorry. And never being able to avoid whatever comes next.

'Clothes off. Both of you.'

Nikki is crying before she even gets down to her underwear.

'Everything. And don't think you can fool me with those tears.'

I struggle out of my jeans. My whole body's still aching from the last beating.

'Turn the music on.' That hard look is in her eye, and I can't help shaking. 'Now dance.'

I stare at Nikki in horror.

'And a proper slow dance. Come on, Shane, get a hold of her.'

'Please, Mom, no.' *Why do I bother? She'll only make it last longer.*

'Dance. And don't stop till I tell you to.' She turns back to the TV; one eye on the screen, and one eye on our humiliation. And she grabs another chocolate bar.

I put my hand on Nikki's shoulder, and we both mouth the word 'Sorry', at the same time.

'Nikki!' Mom has knelt up on the couch, and her yell is right in my ear. 'Stop that snivelling. I won't tell you again.'

'Sorry, Mom.'

I'm glad you're not my real Mom, you mad bitch.

She's cackling now. 'Ooh, Shane. What a big boy you are.'

The flush spreads over my whole body.

'You got the hots for my daughter, Shane?'

All I can do is shake my head.

'Okay, that's enough. Bring it, Nikki.'

Not the hot sauce; please not the hot sauce.

'Bring what, Mom?'

'The duct tape, you stupid girl.'

And just like she's done before, she fastens me to the wall. 'Now bring the sauce, Nikki.'

'No, Mom.'

'What did you say?'

'No, Mom. I said "No".' Nikki will pay for that.

'Don't move,' says Aunt Shelly to Nikki, as she storms into the kitchen. As she pours the sauce onto my penis, I drift as far away as I can, though on the outside I'm screaming and the tears are rolling down my cheeks. I imagine Nikki and me are up in the woods, laughing about how crazy Mom is. My teacher says I have a great imagination. She doesn't realise how much I need it.

'Right, outside.'

Nikki peels the tape off me and we start to pick up our clothes.

'No clothes! Get outside and run up the hill.'

'It's freezing out there, Mom.'

I don't say anything, and take Nikki's hand. The hill isn't very high, but I hope she won't make us go up and down it a bunch of times.

'Now, sit down. Back to back.'

'Mom, please. It's way too cold out here.'

'Come on, Nikki. What choice do we have?'

My cousin is sobbing and shivering.

'How long, Mom?'

She's standing in the doorway with a huge grin. 'How long's a piece of string?' she laughs, and slams the door.

I wish I could hug Nikki, keep her a little warmer. But sitting back to back, we can't even comfort each other. 'Hey, Nikki.'

I feel her nod.

'Think we should run Mom a nice hot bath when we go back in?'

'You think?'

'She sure likes a bath. Likes to be pampered.'

Nikki shifts position slightly.

'Keep still, you kids.' She's watching from the window.

'Yeah,' I go on. 'We could really spoil her, you know. Like the queen she thinks she is.'

'What? How would we do that?'

'Mom just loves toast. Mmm, I reckon she'd love to have a piece of toast right there in the bathroom.'

'You've gone crazy, Shane.'

'We'd have to bring the toaster upstairs. Make it right there, so it's nice and fresh.'

'Yep, you've lost it, cousin.'

'And then, just when no one's expecting it, that naughty toaster might slip right into the bath water. Splash! Now wouldn't *that* be a tragedy?'

'Oh, Shane. You're terrible.' But between checking the window to see if her mom's still watching, Nikki is shaking with laughter.

'Perhaps that old radio'll tumble right in after it.'

I look down at the school; the kids are as small as ants. If they could see me now, oh boy. I managed to grab a pair of boxers, so at least I'm not completely naked. But I didn't have the chance to get anything to eat and I'm starving right now. I can't show myself in town. But maybe if I could see Becky? She's such a sweet girl, even if we're not dating. *What are you thinking, you idiot? She's hardly going to meet up with you to deliver a Big Mac!*

After nightfall, it gets much colder than I expected. How am I going to get through this? I'll do it though. I can't go back there. I scramble under the bushes. It's really not so bad.

The snapping of twigs startles me from sleep. And a light blinds me.

'Come on, son,' says Uncle Dave. 'Your mom's been out of her mind with worry.'

'I don't want to come back.'

'Shane, you silly boy.' It's Mom. 'We've all missed you. We're not a family anymore without you.'

'I'm sorry, Mom. I'm going away.'

'Oh, Shane. You'd leave your sisters? And let them do all your chores as well as their own?'

I rub my eyes.

'We all love you so much. Come back, son, and I'll get a nice, hot breakfast made. All your favourites.'

It's kind of like she hypnotises you, and before I know it, I'm tucking into blueberry pancakes and fresh coffee.

ABUSED TO DEATH VOLUME 4

'You all know Kathy,' says Mom, bringing her hairdresser into the lounge.

'Sure,' says Nikki. 'How's it going, Kathy?'

'Just fine now that your mom's gonna let me stay for a while.'

'Kathy lost her job, and her home, and we're going to make her welcome here with us. She's going to help with the chores, and be part of the family.'

I've met Kathy a few times before and she's kinda bossy.

She gets a whole lot worse when she starts doing what Mom tells her; she becomes Mom's right hand. But little by little, Mom starts treating Kathy as mean as she does the rest of us.

'I'm sorry, Shelly,' we hear from the kitchen as Mom beats her. 'I don't know what makes me behave this way when you've been so good to me.'

'Well that's okay, I guess,' Mom says. 'But just try harder now, won't you?'

When Mom is beating on Kathy, she lets me and Nikki alone. She even gets us to be mean to Kathy ourselves, especially me. And I do it. I don't like it, but I do it.

Mom says Kathy's fat and so she doesn't let her eat much. Kathy loses her big laugh, and her hair starts to drop out. She's got black stumps now where her teeth used to be. I start to feel really bad about it. Sometimes I grab hold of my little camera, one of the only things Mom hasn't taken away from me yet, and take photos of what Mom does to Kathy.

'Why don't you get away?' I ask her one time.

'Oh, I can't leave the family. Shelly needs me.'

She does get away a few times though. But like me, she always gets found and brought back.

'That's right,' says Mom. 'You stay in there where nobody can hurt you.'

That's the thing about Mom. Apart from when she's screaming at you, she makes out the punishments are for your own good. I think Kathy believes her.

'Is she locking her in the pump house?' I whisper to Nikki.

She nods.

'Jeez, it's bad enough when it's you or me in that tiny space, but Kathy!'

'I know, poor Kathy. She's just skin and bone now.'

'We've got to help her.'

Nikki scoffs. 'Like you do when Mom makes you drag Kathy around by her hair?'

'Next time I won't do it.'

'Next time you'll be just as scared of Mom as always, and do whatever she says.'

And she's right.

'You disgusting piece of shit,' Mom is yelling at Kathy.

'I'm sorry. I'm so sorry, Shelly. You know I'd never do anything to upset you.'

'Are you insane as well as stupid? You shit into a Tupperware box in my kitchen and you don't think that'll upset me?'

'There was nowhere else for me to go, Shelly. I know I'm not allowed to use the bathroom; I understand that. But …'

'Shut your ugly mouth.' Mom's face is an inch from Kathy's. 'I'll make sure you never do that again. Dave, come help me.'

I glance at Nikki. *What more can Mom do to Kathy? And please, please don't involve me.* I never liked Kathy much when she used to boss us around, but now she's broken and bruised, I feel so bad for her.

Uncle Dave is instructed to set up a board and bind Kathy to it. Then he fills the huge bucket with water.

No, oh no. They're going to waterboard her.

'Down,' says Mom, and Kathy whimpers as Dad pushes her face down into the water. The screams when she's let up after a few seconds are heart-rending.

'Shane, get out into the driveway. Make sure no one can hear.'

I'm so relieved I don't have to watch anymore that I run out before she can change her mind. Kathy's terrified screams go on and on for what seems like forever.

Mom does worse things to Kathy than she does to me and Nikki. She made her travel in the trunk of the car that time we all went on a camping trip. She makes me kick her in the head, and then soothes Kathy, saying: "I won't let Shane hurt you." As if it's all coming from me. She accuses her of sleepwalking into my room, but I swear it never happened. And Mom makes out she's stealing food, but we saw Mom take the pie and put it in Kathy's room herself. It's as if she's trying to make her go crazy.

I don't think Kathy will last much longer. She's shut up in the laundry room almost all the time now. Even Mom knows she hasn't got the strength to do any chores.

'Kathy's gone,' says Dad.

'Gone where?'

'Remember that trucker boyfriend she used to hang around with?'

None of us can remember.

'Well, she took off with him to California.'

Kathy could no more fly to the moon than stand on her own two feet, but Mom is glaring at us, and we have to turn the lie into the truth.

Later that day, Mom takes me into the laundry room. Although I'm not really surprised, seeing Kathy's body lying there shakes me up.

'We need to take care of this,' says Mom. 'You'll have to help Dad sort it out.'

'What happened, Mom?' My voice is trembling, but I want to know.

'Stupid woman lay down and choked on her own vomit. I *told* her she was eating too much.'

Kathy's bones poke through her skin, her face a gaunt mask of fear, and here's Mom still making out that Kathy was greedy and caused her own death. This is way too creepy. Next time, when I run away, I'm going to stay away.

I'm sure I hear voices, and I crouch further into the bushes. Please don't find me this time. I've been gone for two days, but without clothes, and stinking to high heaven, I haven't been able to show myself in town or get food and drink. But I'm not going back. I'm not.

'Come home, Shane.' It's Nikki. She'd promised to yell so I'd know how close they were.

They're not close enough yet. They might go past.

'Shane, where are you?'

'Shut up, Nikki. How can we creep up on him with you yelling all the time?'

That's my cue to run.

What the hell's happened to my legs? They won't move. Come on, oh please, come on.

'My boy!' says Mom, flinging her arms around me. 'You knew I'd find you. I know you wanted me to, you naughty boy.'

'Sure, Mom,' I say, trying not to cry.

'You keep doing this, Shane. Testing my love for you. But you should know by now, I'll always find you. Always.'

I try to enjoy her warm hug as she helps me stagger to the car. Try to make the most of this loving time before she goes back to being Bad Mom.

'We love you so much. Don't we, girls?'

My cousins nod, and I catch the look of despair on Nikki's face. I was going to get free and then save us all.

'Come here, Shane,' says Dad.

Mom is watching, so I follow Dad as quick as I can.

'I'm sorry, son,' he says.

'What's up, Dad?' *Why does he have tears in his eyes?* Maybe he's going to tell me they can't take care of me anymore. That'd be cool by me. 'If Mom wants me to leave, don't worry about it. I can take care of myself.'

'It's not that, son. We don't want you to leave.'

'So what's up?' It's not usually like this when I'm going to be punished for not doing my chores. This is different.

'You've been like a son to me, Shane.' He puts his hand on my shoulder.

'Sure, Dad.'

'Everything okay out there?' yells Mom.

'Yes, honey.'

'Dad, what's going on?'

'Don't be scared, son.'

'Well, now you *are* scaring me.'

'I have to take care of things, son.'

'What sort of things? Dad, why are you crying?'

He reaches from behind and I see his 0.22 shotgun. Dad never takes me shooting or anything.

'Dad, what the …?'

He raises the gun and points it right at my head. 'I love you, son.'

I start to turn and run, but it's too late.

An Overview of Shane's Case

Shane Watson
6 June 1975 – Unknown 1994
aged 18 or 19 years
Pacific County, Washington, USA

Shane was the son of troubled parents. At the time he came to live with his aunt in 1988, his father was in prison and it is said that his mother was destitute. Initially welcomed into the family, alongside his 14 year old and 10 year old cousins, Shane must have felt that he had been thrown a lifeline. Little did he know that his aunt would become one of the most notorious torturers and serial killers in Washington state. And that he would be the second victim of Shelly Knotek and her accomplice, her husband Dave, with their crimes becoming known to millions of readers of the Gregg Olsen bestseller *If You Tell*.

Prior to Shane's disappearance – no body was ever found – the Knoteks had already humiliated, tortured and murdered another unfortunate victim, and they added one, possibly two, to their tally over the next eight years.

Although Shane wasn't strictly 'abused to death', he was most definitely abused and subsequently murdered by his caregivers, and within the context of the wider crimes committed by the Knoteks, where Shane's story is perhaps given less prominence, I want to remember him.

When Shane arrived in Raymond, Pacific County, Washington, his tough start in life hadn't turned him into a mean character. Resilient, maybe. Accepting of erratic behaviour in others, perhaps. But the teenager was popular at school as the bright, fun-loving kid who made people laugh. His dark good looks, which came via his Native Alaskan ancestry, made him a hit with the girls too.

Like many boys of his time, Shane was into dirt biking and music; his favourite band was Bon Jovi. Whenever they got the chance, he and Shelly's oldest daughter, Nikki, would hare off into the woods, where they could talk freely about their hopes and dreams, as well as their anxieties about what was going on at home.

But Shelly stifled their freedoms more and more, and after she stopped allowing Shane to shower regularly, his popularity as the good looking new kid at school began to wane, and he became isolated and lonely.

Allleged abuses to the children in the home included windows that were nailed shut and locks on the outside of bedroom doors. Items were continually going missing, such as treasured possessions, pillows, blankets, and in Shane's case, his bed. Shane was also duct taped to the wall and had 'Icy Hot' sauce poured onto his penis. All the children were subjected to yelling and name-calling, gaslighting and emotional abuse, with Shelly turning from mother to monster in the blink of an eye.

Shane and Nikki were made to suffer the worst of the humiliating punishments that Shelly dreamt up, such as slow dancing together in the nude, and being made to sit naked, back to back, at the top of a little hill on the property. In Olsen's book, he frequently refers to 'wallowing', a degrading process of being forced to lie in the mud and be subjected to drenching with the hosepipe.

Shane made several attempts to run away, but with the Knoteks adamant that he mustn't leave, he was always found, and Shelly would entice him back with loving words.

In 1988, a few months after Shane had found a home with his aunt and uncle, Kathy Loreno, Shelly's bright and confident hairdresser, fell on hard times. After losing her job, Loreno was taken in by her seemingly caring friend, to help look after the children. Shane and Nikki initially found her to be bossy, as she would admonish them for not helping their mother enough. But soon the tall and attractive brunette was being subjected to a range of punishments for not working quickly enough. Her spirit was slowly broken, and she was reduced to the status of a slave, constantly performing chores in the nude, sleeping in the boiler room, and being transported on journeys in the trunk of the family car.

Kathy idolised Shelly, and, utterly compliant to her friend's wishes, Kathy had to be granted permission to use the bathroom. Fearful of waking a napping Shelly one day, Kathy defecated into a Tupperware box. Shelly's fury knew no bounds, and she devised a new torture; waterboarding. Ordering her husband to bind her to a wooden plank with duct tape, the pair repeatedly lowered and raised her, dunking her head into a bucket of water. For her own good.

Kathy endured almost constant gaslighting, with Shelly claiming she was sleepwalking and stealing, including food that the children had seen their mother placing in Kathy's room. After ordering Shane to beat and kick Kathy, Shelly would console her saying: "Shane won't hurt you."

As her hair fell out and she was reduced to a barely-alive husk, along with her dignity, Shelly gradually stripped Kathy of her possessions, such as pictures, records and clothes, and she was confined for hours in a small locked closet.

It is my understanding that she died of starvation and exhaustion, but with the Knoteks burning her body, we don't know Kathy's actual cause of death. After she went missing in 1994, her family searched for her for many years, with her brother hiring a private detective when the police failed to help him. But of course, Kathy was already dead, with Shelly warning the family: "All of us will be in jail if anyone finds out what happened to Kathy."

It was only a few months after this that Shane went missing again, with the Knoteks claiming that he had run away to work on a fishing boat in Alaska. But Shane had gone for good this time, and Dave Knotek later admitted to his murder. The Knoteks feared that Shane had incriminating photographs showing the torture of Kathy Loreno that he could take to the police, and so Dave was persuaded by Shelly to shoot their nephew in the head with a 0.22 calibre rifle. It is said that they burnt his body, scattering his ashes in the sea.

By 1999, Dave Knotek was spending his week-nights away from the family, to be closer to his workplace, and the two older girls had managed to leave home to pursue their education, with only the youngest daughter, Tori, remaining at the house. In the meantime, Nikki, and her step-grandmother, Lara Watson, had been trying to get the police to investigate the disappearance of Kathy Loreno. It was to no avail.

Around 2001, gentle, gay veteran Ronald Woodworth, lost his own property and was taken in by Shelly Knotek. Ron was soon being made to work from dawn to dusk doing garden chores in just his underwear, and enduring similar indignities to those of Kathy Loreno.

It is reported that Ron was forced to jump out of second storey windows, causing broken bones, and that Shelly Knotek burned his feet with boiling water and bleach.

Within a few months, neighbour James "Mac" McClintock, an elderly wheelchair user, was being bombarded with Shelly's attention, and he changed his will in her favour. Whilst initially his estate would go to Sissy, his dog, Shelly would inherit Mac's house upon the death of his beloved pet. In early 2002, Mac supposedly fell from his wheelchair and banged his head, and died from the head trauma. Shelly added yet another torture to the list she rained down upon Ron Woodworth; she berated him for murdering the 81 year old man.

That summer, the Knoteks were around $5,000 in arrears on house payments, and a public auction for the property was arranged by the bank. But, just in the nick of time, they reported that Sissy had died, and received Mac's three-storey house and $8,825. They had come up with the money, and their home was saved.

Ron Woodworth went missing in 2003, and an autopsy later confirmed that he had been murdered.

So what of Shelly's childhood?

Her father, Les Watson was tall, athletic and handsome, and along with his mother, owned several businesses, including care homes for the elderly and a bowling alley. By contrast, Shelly's mother, Sharon, was known to be a depressive alcoholic. When the couple divorced, and Les Watson subsequently married Lara Stallings, six year old Shelly and three year old Chuck went to live with their father in Battleground, Washington, and barely heard from their birth mother again.

Sharon Watson was murdered seven years later, and her youngest child, Paul, joined his father and siblings.

All three children appeared to have problems. Paul, who was to become Shane's father, was out of control, with no social skills. Chuck was silent; only communicating through his older sister. And Shelly was angry and rebellious; nothing was good enough for her. There were hints about child abuse during the time they had lived with their mother.

The young Shelly was greatly influenced by her domineering grandmother, Anna, who seemed to hurt and humiliate others for her own amusement, and like Dave Knotek, Anna's husband was meek and accommodating, and was made to sleep in a small shed outside the house.

Shelly was a liar and a thief, and disruptive at school, which led to her being expelled on more than one occasion, and she was already showing the sadism that led her to murder in adulthood.

She once accused her father of raping her, but a doctor's examination proved that Shelly was untouched, and there was not even a bruise on her thigh. It seems she had made up the story for fun. Despite her accusation against him,

Les Watson spoiled his daughter, treating her like a princess who could do no wrong.

And what do we know of her partner in crime, Dave Knotek?

One of three children, David was raised in Pacific County by parents who were hard working but poor. Occasionally beaten by his father, Dave later said that he had always deserved it, demonstrating his compliance to a dominant figure.

Dave spent 22 years in the navy before returning to his home town, and spotting an attractive redhead at a local bar, his fate fell into the hands of an abusive and manipulative woman. As the couple grew closer, Dave felt his twice-divorced girlfriend's two daughters needed a father, and being head over heels in love with Shelly, he was happy to oblige. Shelly and Dave had another daughter together, and Dave worked long hours in the construction industry to support the family.

The Knoteks' crimes were uncovered in 2003, when the authorities finally listened to reports being made about them, and Ron Woodworth's body was discovered on the property.

David Knotek was convicted of murdering Shane Watson, and was released on parole in 2016, after serving 12 years.

Initially charged with murder in the first degree, Michelle 'Shelly' Knotek took the Alford Plea, meaning that she pled guilty whilst maintaining her innocence. She was then sentenced to 22 years for second-degree murder and manslaughter for the deaths of Kathy Loreno and Ronald Woodworth. She was released in November 2022, after serving 18 years of her sentence.

Rest Safely in Peace, Shane

Acceptance of Abuse

Shane's story, and the wider story of Shelly Knotek, highlights how some perpetrators can easily fool their victims into accepting abuse and torture as part of the norm. Knotek's daughters were brainwashed from birth, and were constantly kept on the back foot by her gaslighting, lurching between bombarding them with her version of love, and punishing them mercilessly.

Shane was the least taken in by Shelly's antics. Although a fun-loving and respectful boy, Shane had been brought up on the streets of Tacoma, Washington, and had had to learn how to fend for himself, and to keep his wits about him. Despite his difficult start in life, he had at least been spared indoctrination by Shelly from infancy, and he rebelled more frequently than her birth children. Though in the end, of course, he paid the ultimate price.

Dave Knotek is a prime example of someone who accepts the abuse he witnesses, participating when called upon to do so. I find him a bit of an enigma. Being reasonably attractive and hard working, he doesn't appear to have been a person who would have struggled to meet a decent woman, and yet he cleaved to Shelly as if she were a goddess, overlooking all her flaws. Having said that, she clearly weaved her magic spell on more people than just Dave; her murder victims are testament to that.

Unable to see through her many façades, he believed her to be the ideal mother and, if I'm not mistaken, was taken in by her pretence at having cancer, waiting patiently outside in the car while his wife spent hours with her physician. (Or as Gregg Olsen suggests, while she went out the back door and visited the beauty salon.)

It seems that Shelly was mean to her husband too. Exhausted from a three-hour drive to his construction job and back, she would berate him on his return, and on occasion, he took to sleeping in his truck to avoid the arguments. Whilst his wife belittled him for being a lousy husband and father, despite his long hours working to keep the family afloat, Dave Knotek was writing her cards with words such as:

"I'm married to an angel. Your eyes are the kindest eyes that I have ever seen. You love and care about everything."

and: "I feel your love for me even though I don't deserve it. I love you ever so much forever and ever."

Blaming himself for all the troubles within the family, Dave felt that by being out at work so much, he wasn't matching up to Shelly's commitment to raising the children. "She was 100% Mom and then some." And yet,

Dave Knotek later admitted that although he didn't have the strength to up and leave his wife, he sometimes hoped that she would be the one to leave. Perhaps beneath a blanket of denial, there was a man who, in spite of defending her to the nth degree, knew that his wife was not all she seemed.

I would imagine that when out of Shelly's grasp, the light began to flicker through and that he could finally face the truth. So much so, that when his former wife's release from prison looked possible, he took out a protective (restraining) order against her.

Without Dave Knotek's acceptance of his wife's behaviour, I suspect that she would not have tortured and murdered so easily. But I also feel that Shelly would soon have found another man who would confirm her deluded self belief that she was a loving wife and mother.

The Bit in the Middle

Before we carry on with the stories, I'd like to invite you to **join my Readers' List**, by picking up your free ebook overleaf.

Because my books are so sad, I'll also send a quick email to ask you to confirm your place. Just answer Yes or No.

If you don't receive the email, please check Spam – I won't add you without your reply.

Members get special offers, along with each new release at the subscriber price, the chance to suggest children to include, and lots more.

So get your free ebook overleaf, and after that I'll briefly share my ideas on prevention and warning signs.

Then it's back to the children's stories.

Pick Up Your Free Ebook

Isaiah Torres was just six years old when he was abused to death in the most appalling way.

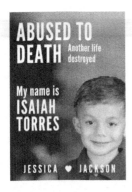

Just scan this code:

Or use this link:

https://BookHip.com/VNGMZJJ

Don't forget to click Yes or No on your quick email to confirm – it looks like this:

Yes thanks, I'd love to join, Jess

OR

No, I won't join just now, Jess

Can We Prevent These Murders?

There are no easy solutions, but these are my own views, which I cover in the pages of my books, echoing the advice of the World Health Organisation (WHO).

1 - End physical discipline of children
2 - Regulate homeschooling effectively
3 - An outlet for caregivers' anger
4 - Listen to the children when they report abuse
5 - Improve communication between agencies
6 - Safe places for unwanted babies
7 - Educate the parents of the future:
   • that a baby communicates by crying
   • how to give love, safety and guidance
   • about bladder & bowel habits of children

In an ideal world, children would not be brought into an environment where drugs and/or violence abound, or where they are unwanted, or are wanted only to meet the impossible-to-meet needs of a parent. But to protect the ones who are already born, we need adequate support, education and a joined-up system where an abused child does not fall through the cracks.

Warning Signs of Abuse

There are various factors that might suggest a child is being abused. This list has been compiled by the NSPCC, but is by no means exhaustive:

- unexplained changes in behaviour or personality
- becoming withdrawn or anxious
- becoming uncharacteristically aggressive
- lacking social skills and having few friends
- poor bonding or relationship with a parent
- knowledge of adult issues inappropriate for their age
- running away or going missing
- wearing clothes which cover their body

And I would add:

- marks and bruises on the body
- being secretive
- stealing (often food)
- weight loss
- inappropriate clothing
- poor hygiene / unkempt appearance
- tiredness
- inability to concentrate
- being overly eager to please the adult
- the child telling you that they're being hurt
- a non-verbal child showing you that they're being hurt

- the adult removing the child from school after they have come under suspicion

If you suspect an adult of abusing a child, don't unquestioningly accept what they say, but instead:

A - Assume nothing

B - Be vigilant

C - Check everything

D - Do something

Listen to the children and report what you see:

To report child abuse in the USA & Canada

The National Child Abuse Hotline:1-800-422-4453
If a child is in immediate danger, call 911

To report child abuse in the UK

For adults, call the NSPCC on 0808 800 5000
For children, call Childline on 0800 1111
Or if there is risk of imminent danger, ring 999

To report child abuse in Australia

The National Child Abuse Reportline: 131-478
Children, call: 1800-55-1800
If a child is in immediate danger, call 000

And by the way ...

Thanks To You

I donate royalties from my books to child protection charities – so far we've donated to: Prevent Child Abuse (US), NSPCC (UK) and UNICEF (worldwide).

I know that many of you will already be donating to children's charities yourselves, but I'd like to thank you for reading my books and helping me to protect children just a little more.

If you have any child protection charities to suggest, please just let me know.

Ready to carry on?

Greedy

I stand at the edge of the circle, pretending not to watch the other children playing. One of the bigger boys puts out his tongue and then turns his back on me again. I shrug my shoulders, and make for the tiny passage between the kitchens and the 'special' classroom. This is my place. Somewhere I can go where no one can find me.

But for the first time ever, someone else is sitting in my place, back against the kitchen wall. It looks like one of the big kids. Though everyone's bigger than me. She hears me and looks up.

'Oh, hi,' she says.

I stay at the opening. Near the bins. *What is she doing here?*

I always feel tired in the afternoon. I gaze out of the window at the school gates, and imagine walking out of here, walking and walking all the way into Coventry. I'd go and have a chocolate milkshake, and … oh there's the girl I just saw in the passage. She's skipping out of the playground holding the hand of a big lady in a red coat. Her mummy doesn't seem to be shouting at her or anything. I wonder why she's getting out of school early. Maybe she's got a doctor's appointment.

I think the teacher must have asked me a question.

'Come on, Daniel. We all know this by now. What letter comes next after B?'

'D, Miss.'

Everybody laughs.

Why did I say that? I know my alphabet, even when I'm half asleep.

'Anyone else? Yes, Laura?'

'C, Miss. *Then* it's D.'

'Well done, Laura. Now, who can tell me what comes after that?'

'Not Danny, Miss!'

A snigger goes round the room.

'Now, come on, Class. That's not fair.'

Everyone is looking at me. I try to make myself look even smaller, and I know I've gone red.

The following lunchtime I run to the passage. I open the kitchen bin and reach in. Half a pancake! But a shadow falls across the opening. I look up and the dark girl smiles at me as she squeezes in. I turn my back, stuffing the pancake down and swallowing the little bits of dirt.

'Hi, I'm Tasha,' she says. But I don't reply.

That afternoon, the teacher brings some of the big kids into our class, because they have to learn about helping people.

'Listen, everyone. I want you to help your partner to draw a house. Give them encouragement when they need it, but don't take over.'

She's there; the dark girl from the passage. Tasha. But she gets partnered with another boy, and I get a boy called Oscar. He laughs at me and tells me I can't even hold the crayon right.

We're supposed to draw a family, so I draw my sister giving me a cuddle.

'What's that supposed to be?' says Oscar. 'That's rubbish!'

Tasha looks up. 'Stop laughing! He's doing a good picture.'

'Shut up,' says Oscar, shoving my arm so that I draw a big line across the middle of the page.

'Look what you've done!' he laughs. 'You're useless.'

Our two classes stay together for story time – it's Little Red Riding Hood – and Tasha sits on the floor next to me.

After a few minutes, my head starts to droop against her shoulder. She nudges me gently.

'No!' I shout. I was dreaming that the Big Bad Wolf was coming to get me.

The teacher pauses and then carries on with the story.

'What's your name?' whispers Tasha. But the bell goes and I dash away because Mummy might be waiting.

The following day, she's already there in the little passage. She looks up with a big smile. I glance at the bin but she's blocking the way.

'You didn't tell me your name,' she says.

'Danny.'

'Do you know 'Stone Paper Scissors'?'

I shake my head.

'Come on, I'll show you.'

When my tummy rumbles, she scowls and asks if I've been to the cafeteria.

'Of course,' I say. But she gives me a piece of her chocolate anyway and it's like heaven.

Tasha doesn't speak Polish, and my English still isn't perfect, but with pointing and smiles, she manages to teach me the game. We almost miss the bell for afternoon lessons.

I'm glad Tasha's not there when I get back to the passage on Monday. I've forgotten how to play that game, and I don't feel like speaking or smiling. But there's something that looks like mashed potato when I lift the bin lid and I manage to scoop some out with my fingers.

'Danny!' says Tasha as she appears at the end of the passage. 'Danny, what are you doing?'

She comes towards me and I try to gobble the last of the potato.

She's too quick, and grabs my wrist. 'What are you doing?'

'Mine,' I shout, and shovel it in.

'But Danny, that's gross. You should get your lunch in the cafeteria with the rest of us. Your mummy would go mad if she knew what you were doing!'

I can't stop my tears. 'I was hungry.'

She shrugs and sits down, then opens a can of cola and passes it to me. 'Want a drink?'

I try not to snatch it. It tastes lovely.

'Can I have it back now?' But she doesn't look angry. 'Don't you have any friends, Danny?'

It's my turn to shrug. 'Do you, Tasha?'

'Not really. They don't like me because I'm fat.'

'You're not fat, Tasha.'

'You want some chocolate?'

'You have chocolate? Again?'

She snaps the bar in half and I close my eyes as I try to let it melt in my mouth and slide down.

'Thank you, Tasha. You're good friend.'

'I'll get more tomorrow. And I'm going to McDonald's after school. It's my sister's birthday.'

'McDonald's. For the nice food.'

'You are funny, Danny. Yes, of course, for the nice food!'

'When I'm older I go to McDonald's for food.'

She's laughing at me now. 'Oh Danny, you're so funny!'

My sleeve has slipped down to my elbow.

'What are those bruises, Danny?'

I pull my sleeves down quickly. 'I fall. All the time.'

'Happy Birthday to you.

Happy Birthday to you.

Happy Birthday dear Mi-iss

Happy Birthday to you.'

'Thank you everyone,' says my teacher, as she brings out an enormous chocolate cake from the big cupboard that you can walk inside.

My mouth waters, and I wonder if she's going to give us a piece.

'Line up, everyone,' she says, picking up a large knife.

We push each other in the queue, sticking out our elbows, wanting to be first.

'Settle down, class! There's enough for everyone!' says the teacher.

But what if there isn't? What if there's none left when it's my turn?

I try to get to the front, but a couple of the boys push me back.

'You heard the teacher, Daniel Pelka. Wait in the line.'

Now I'm further back than before, but at least the queue is getting smaller.

'There you are, Daniel. Not such a big piece for you; your mummy has told us about your eating disorder.'

I look down at the paper plate. 'I need big piece, Miss. Please, I need more.'

'I'm sorry, Daniel. You'll be sick if you eat any more than that.'

I shoot out my hand and grab a handful of chocolate sponge and cream from the rest of the cake.

'Daniel! That's very naughty! Give me your hand!'

I hesitate until I remember that she won't smack me. She wipes my hand with a paper towel.

'I should really take your piece away from you.'

No, please don't, Miss!

'You can help me clear everything up when we've finished. Now go and sit at your desk and eat your cake!'

I try to eat it slowly, to make it last. But I just can't, and my plate is soon empty. I look around at the other kids and I almost snatch the crumbs from the plate of the girl beside me.

The bell rings for the morning break.

'Right, Daniel?'

'Yes, Miss?'

'Can you collect the plates for me?'

'Yes, Miss.'

She takes the books and pencils and goes into the big cupboard to put them away.

I pick up the first plate. Just a few crumbs and a bit of icing left. I lick it from the bottom to the top.

'Just pop the plates in the black bin, Daniel,' calls Miss, from inside the cupboard.

'Okay,' I say, picking up the next plate with almost half a slice still on it.

'Right, that's most of it done,' she says, as she comes back into the room. 'You go out and play now, Daniel.'

'No, I stay and help you.'

'Off you go, Danny. I'll finish off here.'

The half-eaten cake is still sitting on her desk.

'Thank you, Daniel. Now, off you go.'

When I creep back into the classroom at lunchtime, the cake is still there. I take a paper plate out of the bin and scoop some of the cake onto it. I don't take it all, so they won't know any more is missing, and I go into the cupboard. I remember having cake like this at my cousin's birthday party a long time ago.

'Daniel Pelka, what are you doing?' The teacher stands in the doorway.

I can't think what to say. All I know is that my tummy is nearly full at last.

'Come out. I don't know what your mummy will say about this.'

'No! No, you don't tell Mummy!'

'But Daniel, you've stolen the cake.'

'Please don't tell, Mummy. Please don't tell her.' I start to cry.

'Come here, sweetheart.' She takes my hand and sits me down in the toy corner. 'You know stealing is wrong, Daniel. Why did you do it?'

'I was hungry. I'm sorry.'

'I know it must be hard for you, having an eating disorder, Daniel, but if you eat too much you'll be very ill.'

'Please don't tell.'

'Daniel, it was you that took food from the other children's lunchboxes, wasn't it?

I shake my head. 'No, Miss. I didn't do that.'

'I think it was, Danny.'

'Please don't tell Mummy. Please.'

'Shh now, sweetheart. Let me think about it.'

I cling to her, shaking and crying.

She strokes my back, and I want to stay here forever. 'Alright, Daniel. I won't tell this time. But don't steal anything again, okay?'

'I won't.'

'Promise?'

I cross my fingers behind my back. 'I promise.'

'Good boy. Now, let's get you cleaned up and we'll forget about it.'

'Yes, Miss. Thank you, Miss.'

Tasha's mummy gives her sweets or chocolate to take to school every day, and she shares them with me.

'What is this one?' I ask her, licking my lips.

'It's a Milky Way, silly.'

Ava Marks appears at the opening and puts her hands on her hips. 'I'm going to tell the teacher what you just did, Tubby Tash.'

'Nobody's supposed to give Daniel anything to eat,' says Ava's friend, Sophie.

'I'm sorry,' says Tasha. 'I didn't know.'

'Don't you remember, we were all told about his weird eating disorder? He never gets full, and the teachers told us not to give him anything.'

'Oh. No, I can't remember.'

'Well, it's true. And if you do it again, we're definitely telling.'

But Tasha is kind, and as soon as they've gone she shares the rest of the bar. While I'm eating it, she keeps a look-out in case they come back.

'You not here yesterday, Tasha.'

'I don't have to come every day, Danny. I've got other friends, you know.'

'Okay,' I say. 'Yes, I see you with some girls.'

'I'm sorry, Danny. I'm still your friend.' She hears a noise and turns round. 'Hey, who are you?'

The other girl reaches past Tasha; a piece of toast in her hand. 'Quick, Danny.'

I grab it and it's gone in a flash. And so has she.

Tasha looks puzzled. 'What was that about?'

'My sister. She try to help me.'

'By bringing you cold toast? What sort of a sister does that?'

'She kind, Tasha. You don't say bad things about her.'

'Oh, okay. Want some of my Twix?'

'You very kind too, Tasha.'

Tasha puts her arm round me. I know I shouldn't cry. If they know I've been crying, they'll say: "I'll give you something to cry about." But I can't help myself.

'I like you. I like being with you.' I say. 'Good friend.'

She hugs me tighter. 'I always wanted a baby brother,' she says.

I'm sitting by the climbing frame, waiting for Mummy, when Tasha spots me and skips over to sit beside me.

'Go away.'

'What?'

'Go away, Tasha. Please, you go away.'

She stands up and brushes off her skirt. 'Why, Danny?'

Mummy could get here any minute. 'Please, Tasha. You leave me alone.'

She flounces away and plonks herself down on the grass, just as Mummy strides through the entrance with the baby on one hip. She beckons me with her other hand. She doesn't smile. Neither do I, as I slope after her through the gates.

The next day I can't wait to see Tasha.

'What are you so happy about?'

I roll up my sleeve to show her the bruise all the way up my arm.

'I don't understand, Danny. That looks awful. Does it hurt?'

'Oh, yes,' I say. 'Nurse has seen it. Going to help me.'

She frowns. 'There's not much you can do about a bruise, Danny. It'll just go away on its own.'

'When? When it will go away?'

'Maybe a week or two.'

I breathe again. 'That's okay, then.'

'Do you go to Doctor, Tasha?'

'Well, yes. Sometimes. Why?'

'Do you go with Mummy?'

'Yes, of course.'

'It's okay to go without Mummy?'

'I don't think so, Danny. Your mummy can explain things to the doctor better than you can.'

I think about it. 'Maybe one day I talk to Doctor. And Mummy stays at home.'

'Oh, never mind, Danny. Come on, let's practice that clapping game I taught you.'

Tasha doesn't always come to the passage now that she has new friends. And sometimes when she does come, I don't want to speak to her.

'Danny.'

I don't look at her as she squeezes in beside me.

'Danny, it's me.'

I hunch my shoulders.

'Come on, Danny, talk to me.'

My hand flies up to my mouth then back down again. Half the pancake is still on the ground beside me.

'You're not eating that? That's disgusting, Danny! It's covered in dirt!' She reaches over to try and grab it.

'No, you don't take it! For me!'

'But it's horrible, Danny. It might make you poorly.'

I start to cry.

'Everyone says you'll eat anything. It looks like they're right.'

'I'm not naughty boy.'

'I know, you can't help it. It's a disease.'

I gobble down the last of the pancake and wipe my mouth.

'Don't cry, Danny. It's not your fault if you have an illness. Hey, stand up and let me cuddle you.'

'I'm thirsty,' I say. 'Have you got lemonade?'

'Yeah, I've got a can of cola today. I spent my own pocket money on it. Here, would you like a drink?'

I nod. I've drunk as much as I can from the taps but I'm thirsty again.

'Danny, hang on. We were going to share it.'

I wipe my mouth with the back of my hand. 'Sorry, Tasha.'

'S'okay, I suppose. Hey, your mummy looks nice. I saw her picking you up the other day.'

'My daddy is nice,' he says. 'My real daddy, in Poland. He give me Teddy.'

'My real daddy died.'

'Oh. Do you have new daddy?'

'Yes, he's called Tony.'

'Do you like him?'

'He's okay.'

'Do you sleep in bed?'

'What do you mean, Danny? Of course I do. Don't you?'

I hesitate. 'Of course. And what about meal? Do you eat meal? Every night?'

'If you're going to say silly things, I'm going to go and play with my other friends.'

'No, stay. Please, stay.'

'Only if you stop asking daft questions.'

'One more.'

Tasha shrugs. 'Okay, then.'

'Who beat you most; Mummy or Stepdaddy?'

She shakes her head. 'I said no more silly questions. Come on, lets play 3-6-9.'

In the middle of the game, my sister appears at the entrance again and I jump up. As quick as lightning, she's given me a hug, put something in my pocket, and vanished again.

'That's your sister? She's not very friendly.'

I shrug.

'Why doesn't she stay? She could play with us.'

I glare at Tasha. 'Not allowed to stay. She bring present.'

I put my hand in my pocket and bring out a potato waffle. I could smell them cooking last night.

'Danny, what's that? It looks horrible.'

'She love me and is kind to me.'

'She brought you an old waffle!' says Tasha. 'Yuk, what a present!'

'You don't laugh at her. She try to help me.'

I can feel my eyes filling with tears again, so it's nice when Tasha gives me a cuddle, and then the bell rings.

We're not at school anymore. For one or two weeks.

'I'm so thirsty, Mummy.'

'You know what you get for complaining.' She drags me down to the kitchen. 'Get the spoon.'

I open the drawer, and look at the spoon, wondering if I can run.

'Hurry up, Daniel.'

I hand it to her.

She laughs. 'What are you shaking for? Mmm, this is lovely medicine for you.' And she unscrews the lid of the salt pot and digs the spoon in. 'Open up.'

'No, Mummy. Please don't make me.'

'Didn't you hear what I said? Open your mouth. Now!'

I splutter and choke as I try to make the salt go down.

'Mummy, stop it,' says my sister.

But Mummy makes my sister go to her room. And shoves another spoonful between my lips.

Then I have to kneel in the corner for a long time.

They've taken the handle off my door, and Mummy shouts when I try to push and push, and it leaves my handprint on it. I'm not allowed out of the room, even to go to the toilet. Mummy tells me to just use the mattress, but she uses bad words when she says it. So I have to use it, but then when Stepdaddy sees it he beats me because I made it so dirty. That's when they drag me to the bathroom, and put me in cold water until I can't breathe.

Stepdaddy is happy because when he checks my tummy every day it is getting smaller. But just to be sure I'm not getting fat, he makes me run around and then do squats. I feel so weak and I fall over many times. But I have to get up and start again.

I'm glad to be back at school, but Tasha mostly plays with girls in her class now. I don't see her much.

We make something called 'experiment' in class. We are going to grow beans I think. At break-time, I put some in my pocket and go to the sandpit.

'Danny! You can't eat those!'

It's my teacher. Why do they always find me?

'Give them to me, Daniel. They're poisonous.'

'But my mummy has in kitchen.'

'Yes, they're okay when they're cooked. But when they're raw, they can really harm you.'

'Please, can I have apple?'

'Oh, Danny. You know you're not supposed to be eating anything extra.' Then she looks at me closely. 'But you do look quite thin, sweetheart. I'll go and get you something. Just don't eat those beans!'

Some big boys come up while she's gone and call me bad names. They pull my jumper and I start to cry when they rip it.

Miss Bewes chases them away. 'What were they doing, Danny?'

'Nothing.'

'But you're upset, Daniel.'

'Mummy will be cross.'

'I'll explain when she comes to collect you this afternoon.'

'No! No, don't tell. Please don't tell. I will hide jumper.'

'Come with me, sweetheart. I'll mend it for you.'

'You can do that?'

'Of course. Come on. We'll go to the nurses room.'

'You can mend for me!'

'Yes, Danny. Don't make such a fuss. And hurry up before lessons start again.'

But Mummy notices straight away.

'What the hell have you done now?' She presses the keys on her phone. 'I'm letting Mariusz know that you've ruined your jumper. It'll be a punishment then straight to bed for you.' She storms away, holding my sister's hand, and I follow behind.

I try not to think about the punishment. My legs are shaking, and I can't keep up but Mummy doesn't look round.

When we're nearly home, she shouts, 'Get here, NOW,' and I have to try and catch up.

I stumble up the steps.

Mummy punches the side of my head. 'Get in and get the salt.'

'Mummy,' my sister says, but Mummy glares at her. 'Yes, young lady?'

'Nothing, Mummy. It's just, I don't think Danny ripped his jumper on purpose.'

'Have you ripped *your* jumper?

'No, Mummy.'

'Well, he's ripped his, and he'll be punished. And that's that.'

I try to touch my sister's hand but Mummy is pushing me into the bathroom and starting to run the bath.

This time it's even harder than before. I try to stay calm and hold my breath as she forces my head under, but soon I'm fighting to get away and gulping mouthfuls of water. I can't even shout for help. No one can help me anyway. Through my panic, I try to think of my daddy and the teddy he sent me. I think of my sister giving me a hug. I think of my auntie and my cousins that day we went to the funfair. I think of Tasha passing me a handful of Maltesers. But mostly I think of Mummy telling me she's sorry and she didn't mean to hurt me, and that from now on she's going to love me.

Instead, I hear her calling, 'Mariusz, come here. I'm giving Daniel a harsh punishment.' And Stepdaddy comes into the bathroom.

Now I can't think of anything except how much he's going to hurt me.

Please, please can someone help me?

An Overview of Daniel's Case

Daniel Pelka
15 July 2007 – 3 March 2012
aged 4 years & 8 months
Coventry, England

At approximately 3:00am on Saturday 3rd March 2012, Daniel Pelka's mother phoned for an ambulance, and the emaciated four-year-old was admitted to hospital. Little Daniel was pronounced dead at 3:50am, with the cause of death given as a severe head injury. But the 999 call made by the grieving mother came under suspicion of being 'staged', as Daniel had in fact been severely beaten 33 hours earlier and left alone to die.

The tiny boy weighed just 23lbs (the normal weight for a boy of his age being 34lbs). And in addition to the acute subdural haematoma on the right side of his head, that ultimately killed him, Daniel had numerous bruises, and he was found later to also have older haematomas, months, or perhaps years, old.

Daniel's parents, Magdalena Luczak and Eryk Pelka, came from Poland to England in late 2005. Life was not easy for the young couple, and due to their immigrant status, they were not entitled to housing benefit or free school meals for the children. By 2008, the relationship had ended, and whilst Luczak remained in the UK with their daughter and baby Daniel, Eryk Pelka returned to Poland.

One of five children, Magdalena Luczak was brought up in a cramped flat in the city of Lodz, central Poland. As a youngster, Magda longed to be like Emma Bunton of the Spice Girls, but it is alleged that by her late teenage years she had become increasingly wayward, and her problems with alcohol may have already begun.

Following the breakdown of her relationship with Eryk Pelka, Luczak met another Polish national, Mariusz Krezolek.

Born in a village in south-west Poland, Mariusz Krezolek spent a year in the Polish Army, and served time in jail for motoring offences. When he came to England, he found work in a car manufacturing plant in Coventry, and met the young mother of two small children. The pair set up home early in 2010. Krezolek began his reign of terror almost immediately, and is said to have described his stepson as "retarded", saying to his work-mates: "It's not even worth beating him because he won't feel pain as he's autistic."

Within a year, Daniel had suffered a broken arm, requiring surgery. When he was admitted to hospital, the consultant was suspicious of his mother's explanation that Daniel had fallen from a sofa. Concerned about the time lapse between the child's injury and his presentation at the hospital, the doctor alerted Child Protection Services. Luczak became extremely angry when she was informed of the investigation, raging at medical staff at a follow-up appointment: "In Poland when a child breaks his arm, the doctors look at the child, not the parents". The family, (including Daniel's elder sibling, who was forced to do so) repeated to the authorities that the two-year-old had fallen off the sofa. The inquiry by the police and social services came to a halt five months later, when deliberate harm could not be proved.

Later that year, his mother told a health visitor that Daniel had an excessive appetite, but in fact, the campaign to beat and starve her son was already well under way.

Daniel started at Little Heath Primary School in September 2011, and although at first he seemed to be "smart and well cared for", staff soon had reason to be concerned. His class teacher felt that he was not interacting well with the other pupils, and was not making the progress she expected. She noticed that Daniel was in the habit of eating as many as five pieces of fruit every day, from the bowl that was available to the children. At a meeting with Daniel and his mother, she observed that Luczak was stern with her son and "barely looked at him", and that she claimed, on this and several other occasions, that they had a doctor's appointment pending, to discuss his "excessive eating habits".

At the trial of Luczak and Krezolek at Birmingham Crown Court, school staff were in tears as they recalled being told by his mother that Daniel suffered from a rare eating disorder which made him greedy, and that they shouldn't feed him. When the desperate little boy tried to steal food at school, staff gently scolded him, and tried to explain that what he was doing was wrong, then resorted to locking up the other children's lunch-boxes, as Daniel would try to take food from them. The little boy sought food in the rubbish bins, picking out the core of an apple or a pear, and attempting to get the last bit of yoghurt out of an empty pot. Staff witnessed the starving boy eating muddy pancakes from the ground, eating almost half of a large birthday cake, and heart-breakingly, on the last day he attended school, trying to shell and eat the dried kidney beans that were part of a classroom experiment.

Luczak had also told staff that Daniel had inherited a genetic learning disability from his father, which was another lie.

His teacher recorded her worries about Daniel in the school's concerns book, including the appearance of four dot-shaped bruises around the side of his neck, which we may now assume to be strangulation marks.

Unbeknownst to his teachers, when not at school, Daniel was being tortured by his mother and stepfather. He was kept locked in a small room (containing only a urine- and faeces-stained mattress, which he was made to use as a toilet), force-fed with salt, subjected to drowning, and repeatedly beaten. The door handle of the box room where he was imprisoned had been removed so that he could not escape, and poignantly, a child's handprint was discerned in the place where the handle should have been.

Daniel attended school only two thirds of the time, and an educational welfare officer, along with a school nurse, visited Daniel's home on several occasions, with Luczak then texting Krezolek: "I was telling you I'd be having problems and a punishment because he's not at school. The hags from the council were here!"

The school nurse referred Daniel to a paediatrician, who was again told that Daniel (who was not spoken to during the appointment), had an insatiable appetite and was aggressive towards anyone who denied him food. The doctor felt that the little boy could be suffering from a hypermetabolic disorder, as well as being on the autistic spectrum. He ensured that blood tests were undertaken and referred him to a consultant.

When Daniel returned to school after the February half-term break in 2012, he was said to be lethargic, "looking like an old man" with sunken eyes, and he appeared to be "sad, desperate and lonely" as he ate dried beans in the sand-pit. His teacher also reported seeing him with two black eyes and a scratched nose.

A few weeks before his death, the deputy headteacher rang Daniel's GP to voice her concerns. In a six-minute conversation, she referred to Daniel's unusually keen appetite, though he was losing weight, and the paleness of his skin. Although it was extremely rare for a teacher to make such a call, at a disciplinary tribunal, after Daniel's death, to assess the doctor's fitness to practice, he said he had not suspected neglect or maltreatment. Regrettably, not feeling that the situation was urgent, he merely suggested that Daniel's parents make an appointment with the practice with a view to assessing him himself.

The doctor admitted that he did not record adequate details of the information provided during the phone call and that he "failed to formulate an action plan to ensure appropriate follow-up of the concerns". Although his lack of urgency and follow-up amounts to misconduct, the panel felt that his fitness to practise was not impaired.

Daniel's stepfather, Mariusz Krezolek, admitted in court that he would not have been so cruel to a child of his own, and to compound this callous indifference to Daniel's plight, he seemed to be proud of the fact that he and Luczak had had sex in the two day period between Daniel's death and their subsequent arrest.

He also confessed to feeding Daniel salt as a punishment, and that on at least one other occasion, Luczak had forced her son to consume it when he had asked for a drink.

Krezolek told the court that in the hours before his stepson died, Daniel had fallen over three times in the home, but that Luczak was worried about social services noticing Daniel's bruising, and warned her boyfriend not to call 999. She also told him that the falls could be caused by Daniel's salt intake, adding "maybe he's feeling weak, he'll be all right tomorrow". According to Krezolek, she then took her son upstairs for a bath, where it is believed he became unconscious.

Daniel's mother claimed to be under the control of Krezolek; saying that he would half-strangle her if she attempted to protect or feed her son. She told the court that her partner hated Daniel, and would punish him daily, by making him kneel in the corner, run around, or perform squats. She also claimed that Krezolek would check Daniel's tummy for any slight increase, to make sure he didn't gain weight.

However, with their mobile phones providing crucial evidence, she and her boyfriend were incriminated by text messages, showing that they were equally guilty of torturing the little boy.

For example, in this exchange, on 7 October 2011, the pair are clearly planning Daniel's fate together: "Magda, lead him to the room and lock him there, you'll have some peace and do wait for me."

She replies: "We'll deal with Rudy (the name they called Daniel by) after school, he won't see grub at all. I'm going home now. Call me on your break."

And again from Luczak to Krezolek on 21 October 2011: "When you're going to the shop then do remove Rudy's door handle so (Daniel's sibling) won't be opening the door for him."

On 2 February 2012, Daniel's mother sent these two messages to her boyfriend: "Well now he's temporarily unconscious because I nearly drowned him. He's already in bed covered with the duvet and asleep and I am having some quiet time."

And a few minutes later: "I won't be hitting him but if I hear him when he later wakes up then he's going back to the bathtub. I didn't let the water out", clearly showing that the torture was coldly pre-meditated, and that the starving, half-drowned child was not even permitted to cry, despite enduring salt poisoning and water torture, and many other cruelties.

During her son's dying hours on 2 March 2012, Luczak texted: "He'll get over it by tomorrow. There is no point to stress ourselves out and to call an ambulance because that will cause proper problems."

In common with many other child murderers, Luczak and Krezolek were not content with merely abusing Daniel themselves. The trial judge stated that the perpetrators "carried out a deliberate and cynical deception of teaching, welfare and medical personnel, which was designed to conceal what was happening, to prevent any help being provided for Daniel".

This level of manipulation demonstrates how committed they were to making Daniel's life an absolute misery.

Mrs Justice Cox affirmed that Luczak and Krezolek had "caused severe physical and mental suffering" and that his punishments were "designed to humiliate" in a "campaign of cruelty. What was handed out to Daniel was incomprehensible brutality by both of you". She said: "We will never know exactly what form it took because you have not explained it – he must have been absolutely terrified".

In November 2011, texts sent by Luczak to Krezolek show that she was making sure that Daniel was denied medical care despite him being in dire need: "I'll call this clinic and change this appointment for him because he's even more ill than he was."

A text from Luczak in February 2012 shows her attempts to manipulate those around her, particularly those trying to help her son: "You were striking him by the hands and he's saying in the lady's presence that it's hurting and I told him if he doesn't talk such nonsense he'd get a chocolate bar later on." The 'lady' is presumably either the school nurse or a welfare officer.

Daniel's sister gave evidence in a police interview which was then screened at her mother's trial. In a room filled with cushions and toys, she told the police officer that she would try to get extra food to give to Daniel, who was made to remain upstairs; kept apart from the rest of the family. She recalled Daniel being put into a "really, really cold" bath, with him being held under the water, and her stepfather bashing her brother's head against the sides of the bath.

When asked if she helped her brother to get food to eat, the child replied that she had found a card on the floor and used it to buy food for him, and that she would sometimes make toast for Daniel, but that she had to be careful not to be seen by her mother and stepfather.

From the time of their arrests, whenever the opportunity arose, Krezolek and Luczak were seen to hold hands or stroke each other's fingers, despite Luczak claiming to have been living in fear of her controlling and abusive boyfriend, and each of them attempting to blame the other for Daniel's abuse. On 2 August 2013, they were both jailed for life with a minimum sentence of 30 years.

It is perhaps understandable that Magdalena's mother defended her daughter. Describing her as a "really normal girl", she said: "I don't know who influenced her. I don't know what kind of man she met, what she did, what she was thinking, but please tell the judge that she was a really normal girl". Like many others do when a child who has been tortured to death was already known to the authorities, she added: "Social services should also be held responsible because they also failed the test".

Daniel lived in a household in which the 'toxic-trio' of substance abuse, violence, and mental health issues were present. With the addition of a step-parent who, by his own admission, treated him differently from the other children, Daniel's position became even more precarious. And with claims that his mother had grown up in a home where physical punishments were meted out, and possibly seen as the norm, all the ingredients necessary for a child to be maltreated were in place.

And four year old Daniel paid the price.

Daniel's father, Eryk Pelka, could not afford the cost of flying his son's body to Poland for burial, but a London based funeral director, named Artur Galla, who had no connection with the family, was so moved by Daniel's story that he kindly paid for Daniel to be repatriated and buried.

In the UK, Facebook group, Justice For Daniel Pelka, formed in the area where Daniel had begun to grow up and attend school, did not want Daniel to be forgotten. In a beautiful tribute, members post Good Morning and Good Night messages to Daniel every single day. This is a rare example of people whose genuine desire is for Daniel, and other abused to death children, to be remembered, in contrast to those for whom the story is over once the furore is past.

A headstone and a memorial were laid in Coventry on the same day as Daniel was laid to rest in Poland, on 3 September 2013, eighteen months after he died. His grave and memorials are now tended lovingly by Daniel's family and friends.

On 14 July 2015, the day before what would have been Daniel's eighth birthday, Daniel's mother took her own life, by hanging. On 27 January 2016, Krezolek was also found dead in his cell at Full Sutton prison. He had had a heart attack but had refused medical intervention.

My thanks to Nicci and the Justice for Daniel Pelka Facebook group for their support in my telling of Daniel's story, and my respect to them for believing that Daniel's life mattered.

Rest Safely in Peace, Daniel

In Plain Sight

Most people do not want to face the fact that parents torture and murder their children. There is still an element of shock involved, particularly when a mother is the perpetrator. This plays into the murderers' hands. They are given the benefit of the doubt, and the child may be grossly abused in plain sight.

This is why I keep banging on about awareness. If most people are simply unaware of the number of murders, and think that Baby P and Gabriel Fernandez, for example, are rare cases, they will gloss over a child's injuries and believe the caregiver's lies.

And it's also why my ABCD mantra is so relevant:

    A - **A**ssume nothing
    B - **Be** vigilant
    C - **C**heck everything
    D - **Do** something

Listen to the children and report what you see

Disguising bruises with cream or clothing is commonplace, and explaining injuries away by saying the child fell is another common tactic. Insisting the victim has an eating disorder is less common, but Luczak was able to convince intelligent and caring adults that her increasingly weakened son was eating too much. Looking back, it is perhaps as incomprehensible to those taken in by her lies as it is to us observers. But abusers can be cunning and clever, and as I mentioned, coupled with our difficulty in believing that someone would do such a terrible thing, we go along with the mother's story.

In an interview with the Daily Mail newspaper, Magdalena's sister, Sylwia, said that although her sister had problems with alcohol, she had once been a loving mother to Daniel. Living fairly close to each other, the families spent time together, and Sylwia recalls Luczak buying toys for Daniel, and going on family trips to the seaside and an amusement park. But she reported that things had changed when she took up with Krezolek and gave birth to his child.

Sylwia told reporters that when she realised that Krezolek was violent towards her sister, she offered an escape route for her and her children, inviting her to leave him and live with her. But Luczak told Sylwia that she feared further violence if she left him, saying she didn't know what he was capable of. Thus Magda pulled the wool over her sister's eyes, citing Krezolek as the only problem, and no doubt reassuring her that she would protect her children, yet all the while, she was overdosing her son with salt and half-drowning him in the bath.

Sylwia Luczak blames Krezolek for murdering Daniel, and her sister for allowing the torture to take place. She also deeply regrets not having tried to find out more about what was going on in the home, and feels that she shares some of the blame, but she questions why the professionals who knew about Krezolek's violence allowed Daniel to remain in his custody.

I had originally planned to tell Daniel's story in a stand-alone book, and duly contacted the name of the organisation at the bottom of his photo to ask permission to use it on my cover. Their response sickened me. With the following words: *"Thanks for contacting us – this case is now an old case and as such I feel that it is not contemporaneous to give you the right to use this image"*, they basically said that as Daniel's case was no longer current, they did not feel it appropriate to grant permission. Child abuse, and child murder by abuse, is *always* current, and it does not matter if the murder happened two weeks, two years or two decades ago. Children are dying, and if we have the attitude that a particular case doesn't really matter anymore, then once again, we are playing into the abusers' hands. More than that, it flies totally against the title of a report published after a Serious Case Review into Daniel's murder: *Lessons To Be Learned.*

There were many missed opportunities, and I quote here a number of recommendations, focusing on being aware that all may not be as it seems:

- Simply seeing a child is not protection against harm. The child needs to be *seen, listened to and heard.*

- Treat carers with respect and listen to their information, but always *verify the information* that they provide.

- Never assume that someone else is doing something when you have a cause for concern – two professionals taking action is better than no one taking action at all.

- Parental participation is not the same as cooperation. Don't confuse an apparent willingness to comply, with an actual willingness to accept the need to change.

- Talk to your colleagues to check out practice issues and use supervision o reflect on what action needs to be undertaken to improve outcomes for the child.

These conclusions are chillingly reminiscent of numerous other serious case reviews, including those that followed the deaths of two children that many of us in the UK will never forget for their sheer barbarity; that of Victoria Climbié in 2000, and Peter Connelly (Baby P) in 2007, whose story I tell in Abused To Death Volume 1.

I wonder if we will ever be able to say with conviction that lessons truly have been learned.

Murder By The Book

We are both crying as she prises my arms from around her neck.

'But I want to stay with you, Mummy.'

'I'm sorry, Hana, but without your Dad to help us, I can't afford to keep you. I really can't. I'm so sorry.'

It's bad enough that my Dad just died, but now my step-mum is sending me away. 'But an orphanage, Mummy. With all those new people. I'll be so scared.'

She crouches down in front of me. 'Listen, Hana. It might only be for a short while. When I can manage again, I will send for you. And if not, a nice family might come and adopt you.'

More changes! I hope I **do** get adopted, and when she comes to find me I'll be far away and she'll be sorry.

She can tell I'm sulking. 'I really am sorry, sweetheart. But it's the only way. You're such a good, big girl you'll be able to help the Sisters with the little ones.'

'I don't want to help anyone. I don't want to go.'

'Think how pleased God will be with you. You will be able to pray and read your bible every day. And you can sing for everyone, and they will love you.'

I look at her out of the corner of my eye. That part of it sounds okay.

'I miss my daddy.'

'I know you do, Hana. So do I.' She holds out her arms and I can't be angry with her anymore.

I bury my face into her breast. And we both cry again for Daddy.

My step-mum was right. Things aren't too bad at the orphanage, and I do like helping the nuns. We still get hungry, because we just receive what the Sisters call 'hand-outs' to feed and clothe us. I was never very big, but I'm getting quite skinny now.

'Hana, Hana.' The little ones are calling me to play with them. After that, I'll tell them one of the stories my dad used to tell me. And I'm teaching Selma and Amara how to knit.

Abel is on the edge of the circle as usual.

'Hey, Abel.' I touch his hand.

'Hey, Hana.'

I stand squarely in front of him, like Sister Carmella taught us. 'Want to join in the game today?'

'No, I'm alright. I'll just watch.'

'How's the signing going?'

'Good. Really good. Would you like me to teach you?'

'I'd love that, Abel. Then we can talk even more.'

'It'll be like a secret language.'

'Sounds like fun. Hey, I'd better start the game. Are you sure you don't want to join in?'

Sister Carmella has brought me to her office. It's just a corner of the girls' dormitory, but she has a small desk there and she keeps all her books tidy on a shelf.

'I don't like favouritism, Hana.'

Oh no, what have I done?

'But in your case, just this one time, I'm going to make an exception.'

My legs are shaking.

'You are so gentle and helpful with the little ones, especially the ones who have disabilities, like Abel, George and Matilda.'

I let my breath out slowly. 'Thank you, Sister.'

'So I want to give you this certificate, showing that you are an excellent 'big sister' to the children.' She hands me a square of card, about the size of a saucer or small plate. On it, are the words: "This certificate is awarded to Hana Elemu. As a 'big sister' to all the children in the Kidane Mihret orphanage, she shows great kindness and compassion. We hope she will become a teacher and continue to help children."

I fling my arms around her. 'Oh, thank you, Sister. I will treasure it.'

'Remember, Hana, we don't boast about our achievements, so this is between you and the Sisters only.'

'Yes, Sister.' But I long to run outside and show everyone my certificate. Perhaps I'll just show it to Abel.

Sister Carmella's face is beaming.

'Hana, Abel, come with me.'

I tap Abel's shoulder and beckon him to follow me.

'It's happened, children. A family has been found for you. For both of you.'

The little boy can tell from my huge smile that it's good news. The best news. I sign to confirm it and he grabs my hands and we jump up and down.

'Really? And we will be together?' he mouths to Sister Carmella. 'Truly?'

She nods. 'Absolutely. And such a good family.'

I suddenly remember the drawback. 'Do we have to leave Africa, Sister?'

'You know you do, Hana. All our adopting families are from the United States of America.'

It sounds so exotic. So exciting. A little frightening too.

'Can we show Abel the map again?'

'That's a good idea, Hana. Let's go into the schoolroom where it's cooler.'

Sister Carmella unrolls the map. 'Can you find Washington, Hana?'

I point to the south east of the huge country. 'It's where the President lives.'

'That's an easy mistake to make, child,' says Sister Carmella, and points way up in the north west.

'That's where you'll be, children. Washington state is a long way from Washington DC.'

'Oh,' I say, disappointed to get the answer wrong. 'Will it be just as nice there?'

'Nicer, better. Oh, you children are going to have a wonderful time.'

'Will it be warm there?' asks Abel.

'In the summer, yes. But in the winter, you'll have a lovely surprise.'

I think I can guess, but I give Abel a chance.

'It's white and cold,' says Sister Carmella.

'Snow!' we both yell together.

'Don't forget to pack your bible, Hana.'

'Oh, I won't, Sister Carmella. And Abel and me will pray every night that the other children find families soon too.'

'My good girl,' says Sister Carmella, and hugs me. 'Say a prayer for me too!'

'I will. Oh, but I'm going to miss everyone.'

'I'll send photos. And you must be sure to send us photos of your new family. As soon as you can. We'll all be waiting.'

'We will. And of our new school. And the river. And everything.'

'You're excited, aren't you, Hana?'

'Very. But I'm worried about Abel. He's only little. And with his deafness, I think he likes to stay with people he's comfortable with.'

'You're eleven now, Hana. You are already like his big sister. I know you will take care of him. But be sure to tell him his new Mommy and Daddy are going to take good care of him too.' She nods as she sees me slip my 'big sister' certificate between the pages of my prayer book.

'They will love us, won't they?'

'Of course. They asked for you, Hana. And Abel too. It means they want you so much. And you'll have seven new brothers and sisters to play with.'

Abel and me arrive at Seattle airport and look around at the bright lights and huge signs. And so many people; Abel is lucky he can't hear all the noise! The lady from the adoption agency smiles and leads us towards the family waiting at the arrivals' gate. They all look so neat and beautiful. If I wasn't trying to be on my best behaviour, I'd be skipping with excitement.

As Sister Carmella had promised, as well as Mr and Mrs Williams, there are seven children to meet us, and I drop my case and run up to them with my arms outstretched.

'Children!' Mrs Williams seems alarmed at my approach and the whole family turns away.

'Don't worry,' whispers the adoption lady, grabbing my hand and squeezing it. 'Things are done a little differently in some families.' She raises her voice. 'Mr Williams, Mrs Williams, children. I'd like you to meet Hana and Abel.'

They turn back towards us, and Mrs Williams smiles tightly. 'Welcome, children.'

'Oh, thank you, Mrs Williams,' I say, nudging Abel, who mutters 'Thank you.'

Sister Carmella had suggested I might hug her, but something holds me back. I'll wait and see what she does first. I'm sure she'll want to hug her new daughter. Soon.

The adoption lady is speaking again. 'You can call Mr and Mrs Williams, Mom and Dad.'

I smile and nod. 'Thank you.' *Oh, please let them like us.* 'We're so excited to meet you.' I try to catch the eye of a girl who could be around my age, and she smiles shyly.

'Well, good luck, everyone,' says our escort. 'Someone will come visit next week to see how you're settling in.' And with a wave, she is gone.

'Right, let's get back home,' says Mrs Williams. 'I don't like the children being around so many strangers.'

I squash into the big car between my new brothers and sisters. *My new brothers and sisters!* But after a few miles I start to feel sick, and do my best to tell Mrs Williams.

'Well, we can't stop the car. Abel, pass Hana the paper bag. Abel, Abel.'

I'm feeling so sick I can't speak to remind her that he can't hear her.

'ABEL!' Her voice makes me jump, and I'm sick over one of my new brothers.

'Yuk, she's so dirty,' he says, as I try to wipe it up with my clean hanky and tell him I'm sorry.

'Abel can't hear you, Mrs Williams,' I say at last.

'Nonsense, he'll hear when he wants to.'

'No, he's deaf. He can't –'

'That's enough, Hana. If God wants Abel to hear, he will make him hear.'

That doesn't make any sense. Abel has been deaf all the time I've known him, and we all used to pray for him. Even when the Sisters called out that they had sweets for us, he didn't go running to the kitchen like the rest of us.

'No, Mom,' I say. 'I think he was born deaf. He –'

'Hush now, Hana,' says Mr Williams quietly.

The children scatter to their bedrooms as soon as we arrive. I feel disappointed, as I can't wait to get to know them, but we will have lots of time to talk and play together later.

Our new home is beautiful. So clean and shiny. Everything looks brand new. And now we're inside, and I'm not just looking at the backs of their heads, I can see how handsome my new daddy is, and that my new mommy is neat and pretty. I decide that I'll do whatever it takes to make them both proud of me.

I take Abel's hand. 'Thank you for adopting us, Mr and Mrs Williams.'

They both nod.

'Now, Hana,' says Mr Williams. 'You were extremely badly behaved on the journey home. I can't believe you vomited all over your new brother. But worse than that. Much much worse than that. You cheeked your Mommy.'

'I didn't mean to, Sir. I'm sorry.'

'Sorry is good, but it doesn't change things. We don't cheek our elders in this family. Children obey God and their parents in everything. Do you understand me, Hana?'

'I–I think so, Sir.'

'It's an easy question. Do you understand or not?'

'Yes, I understand.'

'And the punishment for your first offence is just two lashes with the belt.' And he starts to unbuckle his trousers.

I know what's under there and I'm terrified he's going to show me.

'Bend over.'

I hesitate. I've been smacked before, but only ever on my hand. I stretch it out to him hopefully.

'That's another lash, Hana. Now, bend over.'

And I have no choice but to do as he says, thankful that only he, Mrs Williams and Abel are present.

'There now,' says Mr Williams. 'Carri, show the children where they're going to sleep.'

We follow Mrs Williams around the house, as she shows us our bedrooms and bathrooms, which are the loveliest rooms I've ever seen. Although it's been a shaky start, I feel I'm going to be happy here. I'm going to make everyone love me.

'Can I help to make supper, Mom?'

'That's all taken care of. My daughters will be preparing it right now.'

'But, I'm ...' *I'm your daughter too now, Mommy. I want to be your loving daughter.*

'Hana, please. Don't contradict me. You must mind your manners.'

'I'm sorry, Mom. Shall I take Abel to play in the garden?'

'Very well. For a few minutes.'

'Thank you, Mommy. And we'll be good. I promise.'

Of course, we are used to saying 'grace' before we eat, but the prayer seems to last so much longer when the delicious smell of potatoes and chicken and greens is wafting up from the table. I have to kick Abel to stop him from sneaking a small potato while everyone's eyes are closed.

When the prayer is finally over, I pick up my knife and fork but Mrs Williams raises her finger and scowls at me. 'Mr Williams eats first,' she says.

My heart sinks. *Do we have to wait until he's finished his meal?* I'm relieved that once Mr Williams has eaten his first mouthful and nodded his approval, we're given the signal to go ahead.

'This is lovely,' I say, with the taste of chicken and gravy tingling in my mouth.

'Hana!' says Mrs Williams. 'No talking with your mouth full!'

'I'm so sorry, Mommy. It's just so delicious.'

'Very well. But we don't usually talk at the table unless Daddy starts the conversation.'

I'm determined to please my new parents. 'Thank you for explaining, Mommy. I'm sorry for being disrespectful, Daddy.'

'That's alright, Hana,' says Mr Williams. 'We'll say no more about it. But it seems you have a lot to learn.'

'Thank you for teaching me, Daddy. And Mommy.'

I think – at least I hope – I see Mommy smile. Thank goodness. I can do this. I can make them love me.

My new family likes to pray. A lot. Praying before meals, after meals, at bedtime, in the morning, and so many other times in between. We pray even more than the Sisters did. I don't mind, because I love to pray, but the prayers are so different from what I'm used to. The Sisters were always praising God with their hearts filled with love, and they prayed for him to help the poor and the troubled. But Mom and Dad seem to believe that God is cruel and vengeful, and watches every little thing that children do. And he tells them to punish us severely and often. But that's okay. Because I'm going to be so good that I'll never be spanked again.

When Sunday comes, we all get ready to go to Church. I've been looking forward to this so much. I'm wearing a new pink dress and Abel looks smart in a white shirt and red tie.

'Look at you, Carri,' says a lady with white hair, as we enter through a wooden gate. 'With your nine children. You're a saint to take on those little darkies. An absolute saint.'

Mommy looks pleased.

'How are you managing so far?'

I try to listen, hoping that Mommy will say something good about us.

'It's such hard work, Mary. Worse than I anticipated. But with God's guidance, we'll teach them how to be obedient Christian children.'

My heart pounds. I'd so hoped she'd say how happy she is since our arrival.

'They have plenty of excellent examples to follow in your house, Carri,' says Mary, with a smile.

'Yes, my children will help us to show them the Lord's way.'

The hymns have always been my favourite part of church, and I sing my heart out, even though I don't know all the words. At the orphanage, I once won a prize for my singing. At last I'll make Mommy and Daddy proud of me. I feel sorry for Abel who really can't sing well at all, so I sing even louder to drown out his voice.

When we get home, Mommy seems cross. 'Bring the switch, Hana.'

'The switch, Mommy?'

'Dear Lord, don't tell me you don't know what a switch is. The stick, girl. The stick that I keep by the kitchen door.'

This doesn't sound good. 'But Mommy, what did I do?'

'I don't have to tell you what you did, girl. If I say you deserve a spanking, you get a spanking. But since you've asked; what was that unholy hollering you were making in the Lord's house?'

At first I can't think what she means. 'My–my singing, Mommy?'

She actually laughs. 'So that's what you call it! I pray the good Lord wasn't listening to you. You insult his holy name and you embarrass your family.'

I don't know what to say. Singing is the one thing I know I can do well. But I will take my punishment to please Mommy, and I go to fetch the switch. This time it's just on my legs, thank goodness. Although it hurts terribly, I don't feel the awful humiliation when I have to bend over.

Should I show Mommy my certificate? Then she will know what a good, helpful girl I am. She'll know who I really am. Not this wicked girl who shames her family, but a big sister who is kind and gentle.

At least tomorrow is Monday, and it'll be school.

I'm lying on my bed, crying and crying. Because I've discovered that we don't go to school at all. The Williams' children, which now includes Abel and me, are 'homeschooled'.

That means staying at home with Carri, and being quiet and obedient the whole time. The other children, although they seem nice, are so reserved I feel afraid to talk to them. I'd been so looking forward to running around the school yard, making new friends.

Homeschool means lots of bible study, which I thought I'd enjoy, because I love my bible and reading the stories of all the things Jesus used to do. But the bible is different in America, and we're not allowed to ask questions or have discussions like we used to have with the Sisters. And there's geography and history and math and English. But I don't seem to be very good at anything, and am scolded all day long.

When Mr Williams comes home from making aeroplanes at Boeing, I hear Mommy telling him how much trouble I've been.

'Don't worry, dear. It's early days. We will pray on it, and God will tell us what to do. And we can check Mr Pearl's book; he will be sure to have good advice.'

Mommy seems to be crying, and I wish I could go and hug her, but I know she wouldn't want me to do that.

'Oh, Larry. I didn't think it would be as hard as this.'

'They haven't been raised in the Lord like our children, honey. We have to teach them the right way. We can do it together, with the Lord's help. You know we can.'

'Will you punish her please, Larry?'

'Of course. But let me get my supper first.'

I don't know exactly what I've done wrong, but I know that I have to take my spanking with a smile of gratitude.

I want to draw a nice picture that will make Mommy love me, but one of my sisters is trying to grab my pencil. 'Please don't take it,' I say quietly.

'You're rebellious,' she says. 'Mommy and Daddy say so.'

'What does that mean?'

'That you're naughty all the time. You don't mind them, and you don't mind God's word.'

'But I do. I do everything I can to be good.'

'You should let me have the pencil then.'

I hand it over. The picture will have to wait.

'I don't want it now,' she says. 'But I'm telling Mommy.'

I sigh. I know Mommy will spank me hard. She often does the same to Abel too. *Why can't we make them like us?*

Mommy has begun to spank Abel and me with a long piece of tubing that Daddy brought home from the plumbing store. It has a ball at the end, and when it hits my legs I yelp in pain.

'Mommy, please stop.'

'Don't you tell me to stop. Don't you dare, you insolent girl.'

'But what did I do, Mommy? Is it the pencil?'

Mommy doesn't answer. She is muttering, and I realise that she is praying.

'Mommy, please. Please.' Tears are streaming down my face.

She continues to beat me, and I fall to the floor. 'You. Will. Obey. Me.'

'Yes, I will, Mom. I will obey you.'

'And do you surrender to me and your father. And to the Lord God?'

'I do, Mommy. Of course, I do.'

'Of course?' she shouts. 'What does that mean? Do you surrender yourself?'

I scarcely have any breath left. 'I do.'

'You do what?'

'I surrender.'

She beats me for at least another 20 minutes, then sits down in her favourite chair. 'Stay there, girl,' she says as I begin to get up from the floor.

'Yes, Mommy.'

She picks up the book that she keeps near her at all times. It's been read so often that its cover is getting shabby, but I can still see the beautiful photo on the front of a little boy smiling up lovingly at the person holding his hand. As usual, Mommy talks to herself as she reads, marking various passages with her red pen.

I've made the sheet turn red. I have a terrible pain in my tummy too. I sometimes bleed when they spank me with the rubber tubing, but it's never been like this before. I look down and see that it's coming out of my private place. Am I dying? Even though I feel unhappy a lot of the time now, I don't want to die.

'Get down here,' shouts Mommy when I don't show at breakfast.

'I can't, Mommy. I think I'm ill.'

I'm not sure if she hears me.

A few minutes later, one of my brothers stomps up the stairs. 'Mommy says to come down right now.'

'Will you please tell Mommy that I can't. I'm hurt or sick or something.'

He shakes his head. 'I'll tell her.'

I hear Mommy flying up the stairs. 'Get out of bed, you lazy, disobedient girl.'

I fold back the cover. 'I'm sorry, Mommy.'

'What! What on earth!' Mommy stands there, lost for words.

'Am I going to die, Mommy?'

'You'd better not, because you sure aren't going to Heaven. What have you done to yourself?'

'Nothing.'

'Nothing! Little girls don't just start bleeding for no reason. Oh dear Lord, how old are you?'

It's a strange question because she should know my age. 'I'm eleven, Mommy.'

'Eleven, no! I asked for a younger girl! What are you doing in my house? And besides, eleven is far too young to start your monthlies. It's because you've gotten so fat.'

I have no idea what she's talking about. She drags me to the bathroom, tells me to clean myself up, and throws a thick pad at me to put inside my underwear to catch the blood that keeps pouring out.

'Filthy, disgusting creature,' she says. 'No breakfast for you.'

I lie on my bed, curled up with the pain, terrified that I will bleed to death. After a little while, Mommy sends one of the older girls to come and speak to me. She explains that I've started with the 'woman's curse' and I shouldn't look at boys anymore, not even my brothers.

'Will it stop?' I say.

'Yes, in a few days. Then it will start again next month.'

'Can I take anything for the pain?'

She looks at me as if I'm crazy. 'And Mommy says she doesn't want to see you; you have to stay up here all day. She leaves a pack of pads on my bedside table and goes back downstairs.

The next day, I'm scolded for being lazy and missing my lessons yesterday, and get smacked on the legs for not catching up quick enough. And Mommy says I'm not allowed to eat so much anymore.

I'm sad, because that's one thing I've really enjoyed since coming here. Enough food to eat. I'm not so skinny as when we arrived from Ethiopia and it feels good. But now, as a penance for bleeding and being in pain, I have to skip lunch, and while the others enjoy theirs, I have to sit in the corner and watch. It's hard to see them all eating, and my tummy growls. I try to look forward to supper later on. But at supper-time, as an extra punishment for being 'wilful' I am sent outside in the cold, and am made to stand as still as a statue for an hour. When they allow me to relieve myself, I have to use the portable potty that they've placed in the yard.

'Where's Hana?' says Abel.

'That's mine and the Lord's business,' says Dad.

There's a tiny hole in the closet door and I can see Abel's confused little face. I want to tap lightly on the wood, but of course he wouldn't hear me, and Daddy would.

'Ah, thank you, son,' says Dad, as one of my brothers hands him the music player. He sets it in place outside the closet door, and presses play. Someone is reading the bible in a very loud voice. It's the Old Testament. I like the New Testament because it's after Jesus came to the earth, and not just what some old people want us to believe. Then I feel guilty and pray for forgiveness. The voice gets louder, but I hear Dad's voice above it.

'Do you hear that, Hana? Everything we do is for your own good. "Spare the rod and spoil the child." We won't do that. We won't spare the rod. You know why we use it, Hana; to make you obedient and God-fearing. Then you won't go to Hell.'

I try to make sense of the words I'm hearing, because the Sisters had always told us that God loves us and is merciful. I'm not even sure the Sisters believed in

Hell. Not the fiery depths that Mom and Dad talk about anyway. Maybe the Hell of being separated from God. I can understand that.

Dad keeps talking about God's vengeance and I try not to listen, because it scares me so much. It's better to think of my real Daddy and his hugs.

Although there's no room to sit down in the closet, I must have drifted off to sleep, because I jolt awake to the sound of hymns being sung. The volume has been turned up really loud and my head is pounding. Dear God, let me get out of the closet soon. But then I might be sent outside into the cold. And then there's tomorrow. Dear God, let this all have been a nightmare and let me wake up back in the orphanage.

It isn't a nightmare though. It's my life. I thought parents were strict back home, but here it's impossible for me to avoid a beating, because almost everything I do seems to be a sin. I don't see Abel much, as one of us is usually locked in the closet as punishment. I miss him.

I'm very skinny now. Often, I have to stand outside in the freezing cold while the family eats their dinner. I long to go into the warmth of the kitchen, smell the food cooking, and know that I'm going to get my share. I dream about that when I'm out here. Especially when snowflakes are falling. They're not so pretty when they're landing on your skin and making you tremble.

Sometimes Mom brings that book outside with her, and she reads it aloud to me as she follows its instructions. It seems to be all about beating children. I think of Sister Carmella and that time we got a new child at the orphanage who was really wild; angry and kicking. Sister said it was because he'd been badly beaten by his parents. I only half-believed her, because why would a Mom and Dad beat their child? But now I can see that it really does happen. I just don't really understand why.

'We meet him with love,' Sister Carmella had said. Even when he spat at her, she told him that God loved him, and that things would soon feel better. She turned to me. 'Beating only makes children feel angry and resentful and confused.'

'It looks that way, Sister.'

'If he doesn't get rid of his anger, he'll do the same to his own children.'

I wonder if Mr and Mrs Williams were beaten when they were young kids.

We've been here in America for about two years now, and things are getting worse every day for me and Abel. Two years of tears and screams and begging for the pain and hunger and fear to stop. I can't get away; there are locked doors and locked gates everywhere. I haven't learnt anything at homeschool because I'm too tired and weak. When I don't know my lessons I get more beatings, and I cry for Daddy and my step-mum and Sister Carmella.

I've been standing outside in the freezing cold for a long, long time, and I'm grateful that Mom has allowed me to wear clothes today.

One of my little sisters tugs at my sleeve. 'Are you okay, Hana?'

I try to stop shivering. 'I'm okay.'

She nudges something into my hand. A piece of bread!

'Oh, honey.' My eyes fill with tears. I keep it hidden until I'm allowed to go to the potty in the yard. That bread tastes so good.

Carri is waiting for me. 'What are you doing, young lady?'

'Nothing, Mommy.'

'And now she lies to me.'

If I tell about the bread, my little sister will be punished. If I don't tell, it'll just be me.

'I'm sorry, Mommy. I just needed the bathroom.'

'Spit it out.'

Jesus, please tell me what to do.

'Right now. Spit it out.'

'There's nothing to spit, Mommy.'

'Open your mouth.'

I quickly swallow the last crumb and open my mouth.

'You think you're so clever, don't you? Cheating and stealing and lying. There's only one path for sinners like you. Straight to Hell.'

'No, Mommy. Please don't say that.'

'Insolence and impudence. The Devil's bedfellows. I'll beat it out of you, girl. You'll see.'

'Please, Mommy. No more beatings. I hurt so much and I'm very tired. Can I come in now? Please let me come in out of the cold.'

'How dare you tell me what to do,' she yells. 'I'm your mother!'

'I didn't mean it, Mommy. I really didn't.'

'You came into our Christian home, pretending to be a mere child, and before long you were bleeding like a woman. God hates liars, Hana.'

'But I never … I *am* a child, Mom.' I'm so tired my words are slurred and muffled. 'I didn't know anything about the monthly bleeding. And I couldn't help it starting like that.'

'And still you defy me. God, please help me to deal with this insolence.'

Mommy drops to her knees in the dirt and prays. 'Get down, Hana. And pray with me.'

I kneel beside her, closing my eyes and clasping my hands together. But I can't balance on my bruised and bloody knees and I fall onto the ground.

Mom rears up in front of me. 'Disobedient, girl. You shame me before God.' She reaches for the tubing slung around her neck, and begins to beat me.

After about an hour, I stop screaming. Mom calls my big brother to take over the task, as she watches and continues to pray.

Jesus, if you still love me, will you please help me?

My face and body are smeared with tears, blood, sweat, and mud, as I try to crawl out of reach. I know it will mean more beatings, but I have to escape this pain.

'Do not move,' shouts Mom.

All my old wounds have opened up again and as the lashes hit my skin I begin to scream again.

'Leave her,' says Mommy. 'We'll go inside. It's time to eat.'

I don't know how long I've been lying here, but it's very dark now. Someone has thrown an old sheet over me. But it's so hot. I throw it off, and try to pull my t-shirt over my head.

My big brother appears from nowhere, and tries to put the sheet back over me. 'What are you doing, Hana? Cover your nakedness. Mom says you can come inside now.'

'Hot,' I say. 'So hot.' I manage to stand up and stagger around the yard.

'You can't be hot. It's freezing out here. Get dressed.'

'Burning,' I say, tugging at my skirt. 'Need cool.'

He wraps the sheet around my shoulders and I stumble as I try to throw it off, falling face down into the mud.

'Hana! Stop it. You're almost naked.'

'Too hot,' I say, and fumble for the corner of the sheet.

'You're not hot; you're shivering,' says my brother. 'And you'll be beaten again for this.'

I roll on the ground; perhaps the mud will give me some relief from the heat.

'Mom,' shouts my brother. 'What is she doing?'

I hear Mom yelling again, and I think she's spanking me with a switch. But I can't feel the pain, and the sound of her voice is getting fainter. My ears are buzzing and I can't move my arms or legs. I lie on the ground and I think the whole family has gathered around me.

'Make her stand up and walk.' I can only just hear Mom's voice.

Someone tries to take me under the armpits and drag me to my feet, but I flop uselessly in their arms.

'Oh, carry her in then,' says Mom, at last.

As I'm lifted up, the last ounce of strength leaves my body, and a beautiful white light begins to glow in the distance, calling me home.

An Overview of Hana's Case

Hana Alemu Befekadu
19 June 1997 – 12 May 2011
aged 13 years & 11 months
Washington State, USA

Most of us know Hana by her adoptive name, Hana Grace-Rose Williams, but alongside the above photograph, which shows Hana at her healthiest, I have chosen to use her birth name. I understand that her exact date of birth is not known, but this date occurs most frequently and appears on her headstone.

On the evening of 12 May 2011, dressed in inadequate clothing for the weather conditions, 13 year old Hana Williams had been forced to stay outside in temperatures of 42'F / 5.5'C, as she had been made to do many times before. Starving, and in the grip of hypothermia, she began removing her clothes, in a state of 'paradoxical undressing' where a dying victim perceives the extreme cold as extreme heat.

Carri Williams instructed her son to bring Hana indoors, where she attempted to perform CPR. When this proved ineffective, the woman called 911, claiming that Hana had killed herself. The dispatcher then asked why she believed this, and Carri replied that Hana was not breathing, and had been lying face down in the mud, refusing to come indoors.

She added that the girl was 'rebellious' and had been staggering around the yard, throwing herself to the ground, and taking off her clothes.

It was after midnight when first responders arrived at the Skagit County home, and found the teenager's body. Hana had finally escaped the tyranny of Carri and Larry Williams.

Hana's cause of death was hypothermia, along with malnutrition and chronic gastritis as contributing factors.

Hana was born in Ethiopia, and gathering information from various sources, I believe that her birth mother left the family home, leaving her daughter to be raised by her birth father, and in time, his new wife. When Hana's father died, her stepmother could not take care of her, and decided to send her to the Kidane Mihret (Covenant of Mercy) orphanage in Addis Ababa. It is here that she was living when the opportunity for adoption by a family in Sedro-Woolley, Washington State, arose.

In 2008, Hana was adopted by Carri and Larry Williams. Arriving from a poor country, it is not surprising that Hana was underweight, at around 78lbs / 35kg. Though she initially gained several pounds, at the time of her murder, and despite being three years older, she had returned to her pre-adoption weight.

Unwavering obedience was demanded of all the children, and the slightest deviance from the strict rules imposed upon them brought down the wrath of their parents. After Hana began menstruating earlier than the Williams' had expected, she was soon being regularly and aggressively 'spanked' with a rubber tube, locked in a closet, and denied food. Over time, she was not permitted to wear clothing, and was forced to shower outside under a garden hose. And the so-called 'discipline' increased in frequency and intensity over the next two years, until Hana was abused to death.

Approximately two weeks after Hana's murder, Child Protection Services visited the Williams' home, and the remaining children reported the abuse, though Larry and Carri Williams weren't arrested until four months later.

'Abel' in the story, a younger boy with a hearing impairment, was Hana's fellow adoptee from the same country, who received similar treatment, and courageously gave evidence at trial, along with several of the Williams' biological children.

Larry Williams was convicted of manslaughter, and sentenced to almost 28 years in prison. Carri Williams was convicted of homicide by abuse, and sentenced to serve just shy of 37 years. They were also charged with first-degree assault of a child, for the injuries to 'Abel'.

The Williams' claimed that Hana: "enjoyed knitting and crocheting, reading, drawing and various crafts, playing soccer and riding her bicycle."

Strict Christian fundamentalists, the Williams' felt that they were following the parenting advice detailed in Michael and Debi Pearl's controversial book, 'To Train Up A Child'. The Pearls' advice focuses on how to train one's children to surrender to the parents' will and be totally obedient; likening the teaching of a child to obey to the training of an animal, as in the phrase: "use whatever force is necessary to bring him to bay".

The book gives detailed guidance on how to spank children of all ages. Whilst the Pearls do not advocate spanking as *discipline*, but as *training*, and actively discourage chastising in anger, they recommend hitting a child from the age of just a few months, to train them to behave as the parents wish, without question.

They advocate the placing of an attractive object in front of a baby, and when the child naturally reaches for it, as normally developing babies will do in order to explore their environment, the Pearls suggest that the parent says, "No," and then to "thump or swat his hand with a light object so as to cause him a little pain, but not necessarily enough to cry".

Unsurprisingly, children raised in this way, with no scope for independent thought from the moment they were born, often praise their parents and their upbringing.

To give a little more insight into the Pearls' book, they say that parents should "not allow the child's crying to cause them to lighten up on the intensity or duration of the spankings". And that a parent should sit upon a child if necessary, while spanking them, and to "hold him there until he is surrendered". They advocate that parents should "*defeat him totally*. Accept no conditions for surrender. No compromise. You are to rule over him as a benevolent sovereign. Your word is final." And "continue the disciplinary action until *the child is surrendered*".

I don't know if the Pearls are evil people. My feeling is that their teachings normalise extreme physical and mental discipline which stultify a child's growth as a person, and that some of their followers use their advice as a basis for hideous abuse, taking the Pearls' methods to "gain perfect instant obedience", as something to be achieved *at any price*.

Hana is not the first child to be murdered by parents influenced by the Pearls' teachings.

A year before Hana's murder, Kevin and Elizabeth Schatz held down their seven year old adopted daughter, Lydia, and beat her for hours with plastic tubing, because she had mispronounced the word 'pulled' as 'pull-ed'. The resulting massive tissue damage ended in Lydia's death. Whilst caring parents would help their child with patience and smiles and perhaps a little game to improve their pronunciation, little Lydia had the gross misfortune to be placed with those who felt the tiniest 'mistake' warranted a savage and prolonged beating.

And four year old Sean Paddock was beaten with plastic tubing, then wrapped in blankets so tightly that he suffocated. His mother, another follower of the Pearls' philosophy, was found guilty of murder.

Like Hana, all three children were adopted, homeschooled, and their parents had followed the Pearls' advice to excess.

I feel that nurturing and guiding our precious little human beings is much more valuable than blind obedience. And we mustn't forget that not all parents are mature, well-adjusted people who want the best for their offspring. Those who produce (or adopt) children include many extremely flawed individuals, who put their own needs, not slightly ahead, but worlds ahead, of their children's.

I have said this many times, but if a caregiver does not begin spanking or using other physical discipline, it *cannot* escalate to murder, and the safest way is not to do so, nor advocate for its use (and thereby normalising it, opening the floodgates to abusive parents), in the first place.

One of the most tragic elements of Hana's murder is that the Williamses, along with a great many abusing families, believe that they did nothing wrong. A child is dead at their hands and they continue to defend their actions.

Rest Safely in Peace, Hana

Communities Acting Together

As we try to prevent the abuse of children by delving into the reasons why it takes place within families, we have to face some unpalatable truths. Otherwise, things don't change, and children continue to be murdered.

Children who are removed from the sight of anyone who might raise the alarm, as in children not attending school, nor being taken to medical appointments, nor permitted to see other relatives, may be in great danger.

And when whole communities collude in the abuse, the situation is even more dire for the victim. This can range from neighbours turning up the TV when they hear a child screaming, to those who carry out the abuse with the backing of their entire community. We see extreme examples of the latter in 'cults', where both adults and children may be abused.

In Hana's case, it was a *niche group* within the religious community inhabited by her adoptive parents, that encouraged *some* of them to believe that beating, starving, and leaving a child outside in the cold were beneficial practices. Thankfully, the vast majority of adherents to that religion, Christianity, even those whose primary focus for their sons and daughters is their unquestioning obedience, stop well short of torturing their children.

Yet some use the words of Solomon from the Book of Proverbs in the Old Testament of the Christian bible: *"He that spareth the rod hateth his son, but he who loveth him chasteneth him betimes"* (Prov. 13:24), to vindicate the beating of children, and encourage their fellow church members to do the same.

Solomon is usually portrayed as a good and wise ruler, yet he left his country downtrodden and impoverished, married numerous foreign wives, and worshipped idols; building temples to three of them. And his advocacy of chastisement illustrates how disastrous it can be as it proceeds down the generations, as Rehoboam, the son who succeeded him, suppressed his people with violence and cruelty, invoking a civil war that lasted for many years.

Followers of Christianity will know that Jesus Christ did not encourage his disciples to inflict brutal punishments upon their children. Instead, his tenderness for children is demonstrated in many places in the New Testament: But Jesus said, *"Suffer (meaning allow) the little children, and forbid them not, to come unto me: for of such is the kingdom of heaven"*.

189

Faith and religion are a source of comfort and a force for good in many people's lives, but it is tragic that throughout history, it has so often been used for unscrupulous ends, and that over-zealous adherents of various chosen faiths can be intolerant of the opinions of others. But I hope there will be a day when believers of all faiths can agree on this; that abuse and murder of children by their caregivers must end, and that religion should have no part in encouraging practices that can lead to deaths like Hana's.

On a related note, my research has shown me that many of those who were physically disciplined as children, including those on the receiving end of violent beatings, claim: "It never did me any harm." And in some cases this may be true. But it is human nature to deny the things that have damaged us, particularly as children. It's part of our survival mechanism, and identifying with one's abusers is well documented. As an example, after years of abuse, Gabriel Fernandez made his mother a Mother's Day card, just days before she murdered him, saying that he loved her and that she was a loving mom.

And as for me, in my twenties (ah, happy days!) I remember being shocked when my older brother expressed that we were ill-treated as children, as I was in denial about my flawed upbringing. As my brother continued to speak, a chink of light appeared, but it only pushed me deeper into denial, until such time as I was ready to face it. Although anxious about delving into the past, I gradually came to realise that my father's neglect and my mother's narcissism had indeed caused significant harm to myself and my siblings, leading, in my case, amongst other things, to low self esteem, eating disorders and depression.

I hope I do not offend anyone by alluding to the darker side of religion, as I'm aware of the place it holds in many of the good and loving hearts of my readers, who would never ever hurt a child. I explore this aspect only as part of my wish to protect children, and I thank you for your understanding.

JESSICA JACKSON

The Pig-Pen

Kansas City, Missouri – 2015

I laugh at my friend fumbling with the bunches of keys. 'Need a hand?'

'Grab these, Lisa. I think it's the one with the red fob.'

'And there's definitely nobody in here now?'

'Shouldn't be. I believe their lodger cleared out when my tenants got taken to jail.'

'What happened exactly, Jen?'

'I'm not sure. I just know one of the kids died.'

'But jail. Why would they take them to jail? They should be taking care of the other kids. All together, as a family.'

'I don't get it either. I'm wondering if they think they hurt the kid before he died.'

'Really? I thought you said they were decent people.'

'They are, as far as I know. And people get wrongly accused all the time.'

'I guess so. How old was he?'

'Seven or eight, I think.' She tries the door. 'Jeez, there must be a whole heap of mail behind this. Give me a hand.'

We both push hard, and the door inches open.

'Feels weird going into someone else's place. I mean, I know it's your place, but they've been your tenants for a long time.'

'I think I've only been here once since they took on the lease. Never been any trouble.'

I clap my hand to my mouth and nose. 'Oh wow, what a stink!'

'No wonder we could hardly get in. Look at all this crap. Watch where you're stepping.'

'Ugh, that's dogshit, isn't it?'

'Let's just get her the damn photos and get out,' says Jen. 'You got the memory stick?'.

'Sure. But why did she ask you to copy them?'

'Hasn't got any photos of her kids with her. Maybe she thinks she's gonna be away from them more than a week or so.'

I nod, imagining not being able to see my son for a week. 'All these surveillance cameras around the place are a bit weird.'

'Yeah, I was thinking that. But Mr Jones is a bail bondsman, which I guess can be a tough call at times. Maybe the family needs protection.'

I shrug. 'Okay if I wait in the back yard? The smell is really getting to me.'

The yard is as bad as the rest of the place. A swimming pool with green sludge floating on top. Bits of old food littered around, and an unholy racket coming from a pig-pen.

Jennifer taps on the window. I can just about make out her expression through the grime, and I dash back indoors. 'You okay, babes? You look as though you've seen a ghost.'

She falls heavily backwards and I catch her before she lands onto a filthy chair. She doesn't speak.

'Jen, you're scaring me.'

She's trembling and I scout round for a clean cup to grab her some water. There isn't one.

'Oh, Lisa. Oh God, Lisa.'

'What is it? What's the matter?'

She can hardly lift her hand as she points to the screen.

At first I can't understand what I'm seeing. Then I start to make out the filthy pool in the yard, but there's actually someone in it. A child is holding his head just above the water. His cheeks are sunken down to the bone and there's blood running down his face. I don't care about the mess anymore, and I grab a chair before I fall down, and pull one out for my friend. 'Oh God, Jen. What is this?'

'It's him, isn't it? It's the little boy who died.'

'It can't be. It just can't be. They must have staged it, for a joke.'

'Are you ready for this?' She flicks onto the next image. The same boy seems to be tightly bound with bandages to kitchen cutting boards.

'But how can he move? He's held absolutely rigid. I don't understand.'

She grabs my hand. 'Will you look at the others with me? I don't want to be the only one to have these images in my head.'

'There's more?'

Tears are streaming down my friend's face, and she's crushing my hand.

'I'm not sure I can, Jen.'

'Please, hon. I can't be on my own with these thoughts.'

I nod. 'Okay.'

The next one is a video. The little boy is walking around the yard carrying two huge Tiki garden torches; twice his height. Then another photo. Again he's tied up indoors. He seems to be bound to an inversion board, with weights holding his massively swollen ankles in place. I can hardly imagine the pain he must be suffering. Jen and I look at each other, still holding hands.

'Just one more, I promise,' she says.

Another video. The boy is out in the yard in the dark. His wrists are tied behind his back and he's shuffling around, as if in a daze, until he stumbles and then kneels down. He pushes his face into a dish of food or water.

'Dear God, what on earth *is* this?'

'It's torture. They've been torturing him.'

'I can't get my head around it. I just can't.'

'I know.' Jen is sobbing. 'How could they do that? He's their son. How could they be so cruel?'

We hang on to each other in our shared grief.

'What's his name?' I whisper.

'Adrian. I think it's Adrian.'

Lawrence, Kansas – 2011 – Four years earlier

Nana lifts me right up and kisses me all over my face.

'Oh, Nana,' I say, pretending not to love it. 'I'm not a baby anymore.'

'You'll always be a baby to me, Adrian Alexander Jones. And Grandmas are always allowed to cuddle their precious little grandsons.'

I roll my eyes. 'Oh, alright then.' And we both giggle.

'Don't *I* get a cuddle?' says Mommy. And I'm passed along like a parcel.

Nana grabs her camera as Mommy kisses my forehead and my lips.

Mommy always smells of smoke, but I don't mind.

'I love you so much, my little man,' she says.

'Well, you know what you have to do, Dainna,' says Nana.

'I'm going to get clean and stay clean this time, Mom.'

'I hope so,' says Nana. 'Look how happy you all are when you're like this.'

'I know, Mom. But it's so hard. Please don't be mad at me.'

'I'm not mad. It's just, I've heard you make so many promises. And then Kizzy gets left looking after them again. She's still just a kid. She should be out having fun.'

'Like I did.'

'No, not like you did. She's too sensible to get into all that.'

'You *are* angry. I knew you were.'

'That fun you had wound up taking over your life, Dainna. And taking you away from your kids. That's all I care about.'

'I don't know where I'd be without you, Mom.'

'Just stay clean. That's all any of us want.'

'I'll keep trying.' She squeezes me. 'I'll try for you, my gorgeous boy.'

Nana shakes her head. 'Do it this time, honey. Please.'

When Mommy takes bad medicine it makes her sick. Which is kinda strange, because mostly when you take medicine it makes you better. Nana explains that this is a different kind of medicine that nobody should take.

I put my arms around Nana's neck. 'I won't take the bad medicine.'

'I know you won't, Adrian. I won't let you. Do you know why?'

I shake my head.

'Because I won't let anything bad happen to my little man. Not to you, or to any of your brothers and sisters.'

'I know, Nana.' I look over at the sack of shopping we brought back from the mall. 'I wonder if I should play with my new toys now, Nana?'

'Cheeky little monkey,' she laughs. 'Go on, then. Pick out your favourite while I fix dinner.'

Kansas City, Missouri – 2015 – Four years later

When we get back to the car, Jen's eyes are almost swollen shut with crying, and I have to drive us back into the city.

'Will you come in with me, Lisa?'

'Of course I will. But can we wait till morning? I'm dead beat now, and they might keep us there.'

'Do you think we'll sleep tonight though? I know I won't. And what if they release them before we get there, and they do a runner?'

'Oh God, I didn't think of that. Come on, let's go.'

I've never been into a police station before.

Jennifer explains to the desk sergeant why we're here.

He has to ask her to repeat herself twice before he calls a colleague who takes us into a side room.

'Sit down, Ladies. And if you're making a formal statement, we'll wait for another officer to join us.'

Jen nods.

'She won't be long.'

When we're finally all seated, he hits the record button, and takes us through the formalities. Then, 'So Mr and Mrs Jones are your tenants?'

He has to keep reminding Jennifer that a nod is no good for the tape.

She sobs her way through our visit to North 99th Street, and I take out the memory stick.

'It's all on there.'

'Thank you, Ma'am.' He gestures to his colleague to load up the stick.

'Are you parents?' I ask.

'Grandmother to three,' says the female officer, who hardly looks old enough to have kids.

'What you've got there; it's horrific,' I try to warn them.

'We've seen most things, Lisa,' the officer says. But when the photos start showing, she has to run from the room.

Lawrence, Kansas – 2012 – Three years earlier

I'm hiding in the corner because Mommy is screaming at Nana.

'I'm taking them,' yells Mommy. 'And you can't stop me.'

'No,' says Nana quietly. 'No, you don't get to hurt them anymore.'

'Hurt them? Don't you accuse me of hurting them. I love them to death.'

'Please don't say that, Dainna.'

'You're always criticising me. I can't do anything right.'

'Let me take them again, please. Kizzy's just a child; she shouldn't be taking care of the little ones while you get high.'

'Stop interfering, Mom, for God's sake.'

'I've been quiet for too long, Dainna. I just don't trust Mike. Makes me wonder what he was doing to Tyrone before his dad came and took him back.'

'He beat on him,' says Mommy, quiet at last. 'He beat on me, too.'

'That's what I'm saying, honey. You're putting the kids at risk again. I'll have to report it. I'm sorry, but those kids come first.'

'Don't do that! Don't you dare. They're my kids. I can take care of them.'

My big sister Kizzy stands up. 'No, you can't. You're out every night again, and I'm left looking after them. After Adrian was born you promised you'd be a proper Mom.'

'I *am* a proper Mom, aren't I?'

'You were, for a while. But now it's all back to how it was.'

'I love you, that's the main thing. Anyway, Mike's never laid a finger on you.' Mommy spots me and makes a grab for me. 'Hey, Adrian, I love you. Don't I, baby?'

'That doesn't make it okay, Mom,' says Kizzy. 'Can't you see that? Please let us stay with Nana. Please, Mom.'

But Mom turns away and starts packing up our stuff, and we all go to stay with her and my Daddy. Even my big sister, Kizzy, has to come too.

At the beginning, Mommy and Daddy look after us really well. Mommy is training to be a nurse and I've got a new baby sister. All these girls! Daddy gets angry sometimes though, and even Kizzy gets scared of him when he shouts. We keep moving house, but all I care about is being close enough for Nana to come visit us. But I've heard Daddy say he's not going to let her come anymore. I hope that's not true.

'You can't do this to me, Mike.' Tears are streaming down Mommy's face as she waves her phone in front of Daddy. 'A text of all things. Don't I deserve more than that? As the mother of your children, don't I count for something?'

'Mother? What kind of a mother have you been? Drinking and drugging and leaving them with Kizzy all the time?'

'That's how I used to be, Mike. But not now. I'll get my nursing degree and start giving a lot more to the household.'

'I don't care about that,' says Daddy. 'I'm in love with her. I don't love you, and that's that.'

Mommy cries all night, and the next day we move again.

Mommy's friend lets us stay at her place for a while, but it can't last forever, and soon we go to live at a shelter. That's a place you go when there's nowhere else for you to live. We all share one bunk-bed, and it's pretty cool because I get to sleep with my two big sisters. There's a big yard outside and I play soccer most days too. Mommy's taking the bad medicine again though, and doesn't go to nursing school anymore.

When the Children and Families people find out how we're living, they say we need something better. Nana wants to take us, but Daddy wants us back too, and they say he has the right, because he's our Daddy. So off we go again; to live with Daddy and his new wife, Heather.

My big sister Kizzy can't come with us, and she stays with Nana instead.

When we get to Daddy's house, Heather is on the doorstep and I run up to meet her for the first time, and give her my best cuddle. She keeps her arms by her sides and doesn't cuddle me back. Maybe she doesn't like cuddles.

I'm excited to see everything, especially the swimming pool, though it's covered over right now. Heather says we can't use it yet, so I say, 'Okay.' But I can hardly wait.

Inside the house is different to Nana's house. And different to when we last lived with Daddy. There's clothes piled up everywhere, and there's mouse droppings, dirty diapers, and what look like rats in cages. Nana has taught me that it's good to be helpful, so I ask Heather if she'd like me to tidy up. Then she smiles at last. But her eyes aren't smiling; they're glaring, and somehow I feel scared.

Everywhere looks dirty, and we don't even have to wash our hands before we eat. I hope no one tells Nana.

It's quite a big house, and I have my own bed, but after a few days, Heather takes away my pillow and blanket. When I ask why, she punches my face and I burst out crying and hold out my arms for a cuddle.

But she turns her back and says, 'Shut the fuck up.'

I tell Daddy when he gets home, and I wish I hadn't. He grabs my arm and throws me across the room. I land against the wall, and my shoulder and my back hurt real bad. When I cry, Daddy says the same as Heather did. But if I get hurt, I cry. Why would you get hurt and not cry? That's when Nana or Mommy or Kizzy would kiss it all better. Things are different here.

Daddy and Heather don't like us having fun and laughing. When we do, they shout at my sisters, but with me, they get the broomstick and beat me with it. It hurts so bad, mostly when they hit me in my face. When I cry, Daddy punches me to the ground and kicks my head. It feels like a little bone comes out. I'm trying to learn not to cry.

When I was naughty at Nana's house, like the time I wouldn't give my sister her sweets back and smacked her on the arm, I would get sent to my room for a spell. But after a few minutes, Nana would come and ask how I was feeling, and I would say I was sorry and I wanted to say sorry to my sister, and everything would be okay again.

But here at Daddy's house, I don't have to be bad before I get punished. The first few times it happened, I asked Heather why she was making me stand with my arms above my head, and she said, 'Because I can. And that's ten more minutes.' Ten minutes used to be hard. I have to do it for hours now.

In bed at night, I cry for Nana and Mommy and Kizzy, and hope they can come and visit soon.

Although she never ever smiles at me, Heather laughs a lot when she's talking on the phone.

'Did you see what I posted? On Facebook?'

Her friend must be saying, 'Yes.'

'Got an absolute bargain. You can get all sorts of stuff. I can tie the little shit up 24/7 if I want to.'

Another pause while her friend speaks.

'Why shouldn't I? He gets on my fucking nerves. I'm trying him on the inversion table tonight. I can practically have him hanging upside down. See how he likes that.'

She shakes her head. 'Why do you think? Because I can't stand him. I've got the girls to take care of. I'm thinking of getting rid of his mattress; he can sleep in the shower stall.'

She reaches out to cuff my ear. Then she pulls it. 'No, of course he won't be able to lie down. That's the whole point. He eats too fucking much as well. I'll soon get that sorted.'

The friend is speaking again.

'Don't be arguing with me. I've seen you belt your kids. It's just the same. He needs to be punished. You don't know what he's like.' She slams the phone down and slaps my face. 'No dinner for you again tonight, boy.'

Uncle Willie comes into the kitchen. That's Daddy's uncle, and he's staying with us. 'You hurting that boy again?'

'I'll be sure to let you know when it's any of your business.'

'I'm just saying, Heather. He's getting real skinny too.'

'Like I said. My business, so butt out.'

Uncle Willie goes out of the room.

'Can I go to bed please, Heather?' At least when I'm there on my own I can think about the people who love me.

'Bed?' She roars with laughter. 'What bed?'

When I see Heather's tummy grow big, I know she's going to have another baby. Daddy and Heather have three more girls already. I hope this one will be a boy so I can have someone to play with. Although I'm not allowed to play much.

'Daddy, I wish I could see Kizzy. And Nana.'

'Shut up, boy,' he says.

I should know better, but after he just beat me, I don't think he'll do it again. 'I miss them, Daddy. They used to take care of us. They used to sing us to sleep.'

Daddy is big and strong and his punches hurt. 'Never mind about them. Heather takes care of you now. Doesn't she? Doesn't she, Adrian.'

I think of Heather making me stand with my arms above my head for hours that time I took a drink of water without permission, and threatening to make me stay outside all night. 'Yes, Daddy. I guess so.'

'Stop that moping around, boy,' yells Heather at the top of her voice.

But I can't help it. I feel so tired all the time since they've made me go to bed in the shower stall. I don't sleep much.

'Your stupid grandmother and that awful sister of yours are coming to visit, so put a smile on your face. All of you.'

Did I hear that right? Kizzy and Nana are coming? Daddy hasn't let them come for a long, long time. Maybe it's because it's Christmas. I don't care about presents; I'm just looking forward to Nana's hugs.

Us kids are all lined up at the window, waiting for the car to pull up.

The living room has been tidied and this morning I was thrown in the shower. For an actual shower, I mean.

'Don't forget,' says Heather. 'What happens in the house, stays in the house. And don't say you're hungry.'

'Yes, Mommy,' says one of my sisters. 'We know.'

'What if they give us sweets?'

'You can take them. But don't eat them. Wait till they've gone.'

Nana and Kizzy look so beautiful. They glow, like angels, as they walk up the path.

As I run towards them, I don't even hear Heather yelling at me to get back inside.

'Nana, Nana.'

'My beautiful boy.' My sisters aren't far behind me. 'And my girls. Oh, let me look at you all.'

Kizzy hugs me. 'He's changed, Nana.' She whispers, but I hear it.

'Come in,' says Heather, and she leads the way into the living room.

Nana sits down and we crowd round her. She *has* brought sweets. My mouth waters.

'First of all, I have to give you all a big hug from Mommy.' And she cuddles each one of us in turn.

'Send a hug back to Mommy,' I say.

'I will, sweetheart. Oh, I like your Christmas tree,' says Nana, reaching into her bag. 'It's just missing a few presents.'

My sisters snatch them from her, but I hang back.

'Don't you want yours, Adrian?'

I've gotten so used to getting nothing that I wasn't expecting a present. 'Yes please, Nana.'

She laughs. 'So polite. Where's my cheeky little man?' And she tickles me. Just like she used to.

Heather stays in the room the whole time. She doesn't even offer Nana and Kizzy a drink of lemonade. I was hoping that if she did I'd get one too. And Nana might've followed Heather into the kitchen and seen the padlocks on the fridge and the cupboards.

I'm holding onto Nana's legs. Perhaps if I keep holding on tight, she won't leave us here. She kneels down and I whisper in her ear. 'Can I come with you, Nana?'

'I love you so much, Adrian, my little man. I wish you could come with me too. But Nana will always be here for you, and I'll keep you safe.'

'Come on, Adrian,' says Heather. 'Your grandmother has to go now.'

'We could stay a little longer, Heather. I could make the kids something to eat.'

'No, thank you, Judy. It's time for you to leave.'

So we line up at the window to wave Goodbye. Everyone is crying. Except Heather of course.

I tap on the window, but Nana is already in the car. Kizzy looks up though, and I can tell she's saying something to Nana, who twists round in her seat.

'I love you,' she mouths.

Oh, Nana. I love you. So much. But I've missed my chance to tell about everything. Then I could've come with you.

Two hours of being nice seems to have tired Heather out.

'Right, I need some peace, kids. Boy, you looked like you nearly told that nosy bitch something.'

'No, I didn't. I promise.'

'Are you arguing with me?'

'No.' I hang my head. I know what's coming.

She punches me. 'Don't you argue with me, boy.'

My tummy starts aching again.

'Now get to bed.'

It's only five o'clock. But I go to the shower stall.

'Nighty-night, boy.' She laughs. 'Don't make a sound. Get your arms above your head and keep standing up.' She nods to the camera. 'Remember, I'll know.'

And she fits the piece of wood across the door. And it goes dark.

For once, I have nice things to think about when I'm in here.

The sweet smell of Kizzy's hair as she hugged me close. And Nana's whisper that I'm still her precious boy and she'll try and come and visit again soon. Daddy doesn't want to let them come, but I know Nana will try.

My arms are shaking and I have to drop them an inch or two.

'Up,' roars Heather from the next room. 'Oh, and by the way, you won't be seeing those two again. Ever.'

I don't believe her. You can't stop a Nana from seeing her grandson. But why didn't I tell Nana about the shower stall? And about the other stuff?

'I don't think I can stand the little fucker much longer, Mike.'

'I know. I'm sorry, babe. He's getting worse.'

'Banging his head. Asking for this and that. Lying and stealing.'

'I know. I know. Listen, babe, we'll get him tested. Get him put away somewhere.'

'I hope so, because if asks me again for a drink of water, I don't know what I'll do to him.'

'Hey, babe. It'll be okay. I'll make the call tomorrow.'

'No, it's okay, honey. You can take it.' The lady is smiling and she smells nice.

I shake my head, even though it looks lovely. It has sprinkles on it.

'Don't you like donuts, Adrian?'

I look around. The cameras must be hidden somewhere. I shake my head again.

'But you didn't eat lunch either.'

'Did Mommy and Daddy say I could eat?'

'Of course you can eat. I mean, you're so skinny, they'll want you to grow big and strong.'

'What about the cameras?'

'Cameras, honey? We don't have cameras here.'

'You don't?'

'Uh-uh. Not a single one.'

I reach out for the donut. 'Can I have a drink of water, too?'

'Sure you can. I'll go get it for you. Then we'll go watch TV together, okay? Or would you like to play with that train I showed you?'

My mouth is full of donut and sprinkles. I grin and nod.

I take her hand and we walk down to the playroom together.

'There you go, Adrian. You can choose any toy you want.'

She sees me checking around. 'No cameras here either, honey. Hey, hey, what are these tears for?' She crouches in front of me and lifts up my chin. 'There's no need to cry.'

I can't help myself. I stretch up and wrap my arms round her neck.

'Adrian, honey.'

I'm sobbing so hard her shirt is getting wet.

A tall lady comes into the room. 'Can I have a word, Nurse Leslie?'

'Of course, Dr Chapman.' She turns back to me. 'Adrian, how about building a house with the Lego?'

'I'll build Nana's house,' I say, as she joins the doctor in a corner of the room.

I don't really know why I'm in the hospital but it sure is nice here.

Their voices are real quiet, but since I started getting shut in the shower stall, I've gotten good at listening.

'No,' Nurse Leslie is saying. 'Absolutely no sign at all.'

'I just don't get it. It might be the change of environment that's shocked him into behaving differently. Behaving better than they told us. Much better.'

'We'll have to see if the tantrums start up again once he's been here a while. But there's been no sign of anything like they told us. In fact, he seems like the sweetest little boy in the world.'

Dr Chapman shakes her head. 'I agree. Who referred him?'

'Well, his family doctor I guess. I don't really know. Although someone said his parents just turned up with him. At the end of their rope. His notes aren't very clear.'

The doctor is nodding.

'It's strange though,' says Nurse Leslie. 'Mom and Dad haven't been to visit him yet.'

'Hmm, I see. Though if he's been such a handful they might be grabbing a bit of respite.'

They ask me lots of questions, and get me to match words and colours, and I try to remember everything my real mommy taught me. They get me to draw pictures of my family, and I draw Nana and Kizzy.

'Are you happy with your family, Adrian?'

'Oh yes, I love them.'

'And your sisters?'

'I love them very much.'

'What's it like at home?'

I think of Nana's house. 'We play and watch TV and get lots of nice things to eat.' I miss Nana's cuddles so much, and before I know it, I'm clambering up onto Dr Chapman's knee.

'Am I going to stay here for ever?'

She hugs me close and I feel safe for the first time in a long while.

'Not quite, Adrian. Just until you're better.'

'I'm very sick, aren't I?'

'Well, not as much as you were when you first came here.'

'No, I really don't feel well. My tummy hurts. And my head.'

'We'll make you better, sweetheart. Don't you worry. Tell me again about your family.'

'Can I stay here on your lap?'

She laughs. 'Okay.'

'I love my family.' I tell her all my sisters' names.

'That's good. That's great, Adrian. And Daddy and Mommy are coming to visit later.'

I freeze. 'They know where I am?'

'Of course. They'll be looking forward to seeing you after all this time. Seeing how much better you are now.'

There's a little closet in the playroom where they keep the extra toys. If I hide in there, no one will find me. But Tammy, one of the other children, seems to think it's hide and seek and brings the nurse to my hiding place, giggling. 'Found him! My turn to hide now.'

I go to my bed. I'll stay under the covers until they've gone.

'Have you seen this before, Dr Chapman?'

'With other patients, sometimes. But it's the first time Adrian's done it, isn't it?'

'Yes. I don't get it,' says Nurse Leslie. 'He's been doing so well. Could be the stress of being away from his family.'

'Maybe. It's unusual to bite themselves to this extent, though.'

'We'll see what the consultant says on his next round.'

'Isn't Adrian due for discharge tomorrow?' says the doctor.

'Yes, I'll miss him.'

'I think we all will. That smile. That giggle.'

'Oh yes,' says Heather to the visitor. 'And I homeschool them all. It's working really well.'

I prick up my ears. *School? Are we going to be sent to school?* I'm home from the hospital and shut away in the shower stall again.

'I'll get their books out for you next time you come.'

'There's no need,' says the lady. 'I can see you have the right intentions.'

'They're great kids.'

'And such a big family. I don't know how you cope.'

'I've always loved kids,' says Heather. 'And they're well-behaved.'

There's a tickle in my throat.

'And did you say Adrian's the only boy amongst all the girls?' smiles the lady. 'I'll bet he gets spoiled.'

'Certainly does,' says Heather. 'It's a shame he's out now, playing football with his friends.'

'It would've been good to meet him. After that call from the hospital staff, we want to make sure he has a good home.'

'I understand that totally. But you'll never find him indoors. If he's not out with his friends, he's out with his daddy somewhere or other. Boys together!'

I'm fighting the need to cough. Heather will kill me if I do.

'They said he was doing well in the hospital.'

'Yes, I think they did a great job at calming him down again. It all kicked off after the visit from his mother's family. It upset all the kids.'

'Yes, I understand that. Some kids don't like disruptions in their routine. But still, he gets to see his mom and grandmother about once a month?'

'Something like that.'

'Great. That's great.'

It's no good. I have to cough. Just once. A little one.

'Oh, what was that?'

'What? Oh, one of the dogs I guess,' says Heather. 'Can I help you with anything else?'

'I'm doing that. You hear that, Conway? You're not wanted.'

Nana! It's Nana. I'm here, Nana, tied to the board. Please come get me, Nana.

'What *about* school? Who cares about school? Heather's homeschooling them.'

Heather laughs. 'Well, sort of.'

Nana must be speaking again.

'Oh, I don't know,' says Daddy. 'English, Math. All that stuff.'

Heather can't stop sniggering. 'They'll all have college degrees by the time they're 16. Especially Adrian.'

Even Daddy starts to chuckle. 'Yes, they're all little brain-boxes here at The Jones' Academy.'

'And physical ed. Don't forget about that, Mike. Adrian's always running around the yard. Swimming in the pool.'

'Anyway, Conway. You keep out of our business and we'll keep out of yours. Alright?' Daddy's starting to boil up again. 'No, that's final. You can't see them.' And he slams the phone down.

'Hear that, Adrian?' Heather hisses into my ear. 'You won't see your precious grandma ever again.'

She's forgotten to put the wooden board on the door of the shower stall. I listen. I stumble out of the stall and wait, motionless. No sound. I creep into the kitchen.

Where is everyone? I can't believe no one is watching me. With spending so long bound to the inversion table that I can hardly walk, I'm not sure that I can make it to the faucet and be back in my place before anyone notices. I'm trembling, but this is my chance to get a drink.

I've just managed to fill the dish with water when I hear a noise. Someone's coming. I make it to the corner between the cupboards and freeze to the spot. I daren't even breathe.

Uncle Willie comes into the kitchen and takes a can from the fridge. I can see the icy water running down the sides of the tin. *Right, come on legs, move.* From somewhere, I get the strength to scuttle from my hiding place and back towards the stall. I don't know if he saw me. I wait outside the stall; scared it will creak if I step inside. I'm stuck to the spot until he goes out of the room. *I'm in. I made it.* Even if I've been seen, the feel of the cool liquid sliding down my throat will have been worth the punishment I'm sure to get. I hope I can manage to return the dish to the counter later.

'Outside,' says Heather.

'But it's so cold. Please don't make me go out.' *Why do I ever think pleading will do me any good?*

'It's so cold,' she mimics. 'Well, you should've thought of that before you took water from the faucet. You were seen.'

'But I was so thirsty.'

'Aww he's cold. And he's thirsty,' she laughs. 'You know you don't take anything from the kitchen. You forgot about the cameras, boy.' She points up into the corner.

'I was thirsty,' I say again. 'Why can't I have anything to drink?'

'Because I said so. And Daddy says so. But okay, I'll put a dish of water outside for you, you spoilt brat.' As she runs the water, my thirst doubles and I wonder if it's worth the risk of going over there and trying to push my head under the faucet again. But I know I'd be too slow.

'Hands behind your back.'

I hesitate too long.

She picks up the broom and beats my face. The blood runs into my eyes, as I put out my arms behind me, and she snaps the handcuffs shut. I follow slowly as she carries the shallow dish of water outside, and puts it on the ground.

'Drink all you want, boy.' And she slams the door.

I can't walk much now, as my ankles are so swollen, with the weights placed on top of them so that I can't move a muscle. But I shuffle across the yard and reach the dish. I carefully drop down onto my knees, glad she didn't tie my ankles together this time. Balancing is really hard, and I keep toppling to the side. I'm so cold too. I think it's September.

Heather is at the window. Filming me on her phone.

Finally, I let my head droop and manage a sip before the dish tips over and the water soaks into the earth, and I cry. Somehow I get onto my feet again, and stagger towards the trash piled up in the corner of the yard. Maybe I can lie down in there and get warm.

'What are you doing, Adrian?'

'I'm cold.'

She laughs.

As I flop down, a rat scurries out of the trash.

I hear her laughing louder. 'You'd better stay outside all night, boy.'

I sob into the heap of rotting food and dirty diapers.

Why don't they love me? Nana, where are you? Come and get your precious boy. I'm waiting for you.

As the sun comes up, they tell me to go back inside, and somehow I manage to get up onto my feet. I'm ordered into the shower stall, but I can't stand up, so they tie me to the little seat inside it and put the board up against the door. I can't hold my head up, and I'm crying but there are no tears. I know I can't last much longer.

I wish it was all over.

An Overview of Adrian's Case

Adrian Alexander Jones
15 May 2008 – 28 Sept 2015
aged 7 years & 4 months
Kansas City, Missouri

Heather Jones' husband was coming at her with a gun. It wasn't the first time, but on this occasion, she'd had enough; she was calling the cops on him.

The officers who responded to the 911 call knew the family. There'd been reports of child abuse and domestic violence before. Inside the outwardly respectable home, there were dead rats, poison, porn videos, syringes and bullet holes.

Arresting Michael Jones for aggravated battery and assault, the cops took a moment to count up the kids. There were only six when there should have been seven.

The husband gave his wife a warning look, but she wouldn't meet his eye. The Jones' told the officers that Adrian had been missing for several weeks, but could give no explanation why. The pair were then taken to Wyandotte County Jail, and the six girls were removed from the home to a place of safety.

Under questioning a few days later, Heather Jones finally told investigators that they'd find the body of her stepson in the pig-pen. Although aghast at this claim, they duly checked, and were horrified to find a little boy's remains amongst the pigs and their mess. It later transpired that after his death, and Adrian's corpse had begun to rot, Michael Jones went out and bought the pigs, starved them for a couple of days, then threw his son's body into the pen.

In the meantime, Heather Jones, realising that she was going to be apart from her kids for a while, asked their landlord, Jennifer Hoevers, who had access to the house on North 99th Street, to enter the home. Giving her the passwords, she asked Jennifer to bring her a memory stick with photos of her kids saved on it.

If there had been any doubt as to the horrors Adrian had endured under the dominion of Michael and Heather Jones, what Jennifer Hoevers found on her tenant's computer was about to blow those doubts clear out of the water.

I have read conflicting reports on whether Hoevers went immediately to the police with these images. Some say that she was in deep shock and waited a while. Whatever the case, she knew she had to go and do her duty.

The photographs show an emaciated Adrian, neck-deep in the filthy pool. They show him attempting to drink from a dish on the ground, with his hands tied behind his back. They show him blindfolded, and bound to the inversion table, with heavy weights on his ankles. They show Heather Jones taking selfies outside the shower stall, with plywood covering the door, in which Adrian is captive.

Heather Jones seemed to delight in the terrors she inflicted on Adrian, and boasted about it on social media, with one post saying: "I can't shoot him unfortunately, but I can work the shit out of him till I feel better."

With a view to prevention, I always try to explore what makes child murderers act as they do. But what on earth can be the 'reason' for these atrocities?

Adrian and his siblings had a complicated start in life. Their mother, Dainna Pearce, had already proved to be neglectful, largely due to her addictions, long before Adrian was born. Having no experience of how drugs and alcohol can ruin lives, I cannot judge her, but I understand that much of the children's care was left to Dainna's mother, Judy Conway, and her eldest daughter, who I have called Kizzy in my story. (NB Photographs of Adrian with Dainna depict a loving bond between mother and son.)

Though lacking a regular, stable home with their mother, the children could always find love and safety with their grandmother, with whom they sometimes lived.

When she met Michael Jones, and Adrian and his younger siblings were born, Dainna convinced her mother that she was clean and sober, and the children went to live with Dainna and Michael out of state. The family moved several times, before moving to Missouri. It was here that Jones was able to continue the affair he'd begun with the woman who was to become Adrian's stepmother, Heather Jones. Had he found his soul-mate? He had certainly found his partner in crime.

He ended the relationship with Dainna by text message, who then had a breakdown, dropping out of nursing school and back into addiction.

Michael Jones obtained custody of his children, and increasingly prevented outsiders from seeing them, and at the time of his death, Adrian was living with Michael, and his stepmother, Heather, along with six of his sisters, four of whom were Michael and Heather's biological children.

Reports vary, but I understand that the last time Judy and Adrian's oldest sister (who was living with her grandmother) saw him was Christmas 2012, before the most extreme instances of torture and murder. (I have also seen the date given as December 2014; the Christmas before he died.) After the visit, the girl describes the children crying at the window, along with her own tears, as she felt something was badly wrong in that home.

After that, the Jones' simply refused to allow their grandmother to see the children.

At least ten calls, including those by Judy Conway, were made to Children's Services about the children in the Jones' home, but no child was ever removed.

Incidentally, before Adrian was born, another of Dainna's children (not Michael Jones' biological son) had been subjected to daily brutal beatings, and was taken back into his own birth father's care. He had a lucky escape, because Michael and Heather Jones both seemed to be fixated on torturing the boys in their custody. Adrian's oldest sister reports that the girls were unharmed – apart from the horrific experience of being witness to their siblings' abuse.

Two years before he died, Adrian had told a Missouri Children's Division social worker and a police officer that he was being locked in his room, with just a bare mattress, and was kicked so hard in the back of his head that "a little bone had come out". They found evidence of neglect in 2013, but no physical abuse was observed, and Adrian was not removed from the home. Child welfare services tried to give support to the family, but they refused it and stopped attending appointments.

Two safety plans were in place, but these didn't save Adrian. When it was felt that Heather was the greatest danger to the children, Michael said they were not together, but this was not true. If they did separate, they promptly resumed their relationship.

In 2014, Michael Jones claimed that six year old Adrian was a paedophile with sexual predator tendencies and had him committed to a psychiatric hospital. I believe Adrian spent a few months there, diagnosed with PTSD, and was seen to be "lively and curious", until his parents visited, when he became "quiet and sullen". Despite this behaviour change, Adrian was discharged into their custody. Michael Jones' claim of sexual deviance reminds me of Takoda Collins' (from Volume 3) father's accusations about his son. It is well documented that if a child acts out sexually, it is almost invariably due to being on the receiving end of sexual abuse.

Like many abusing parents, Michael and Heather Jones moved their family from state to state, with Missouri and Kansas child welfare departments informing each other when they moved there. But the follow up seems patchy. Despite the numerous calls to the hotline, Kansas found no evidence of physical abuse when they visited. Adrian told them he was forced to sleep outside, and was locked in a cupboard at night. One of the anonymous callers had said: "The step-mom beats the living daylights out of the kid for no reason at all. She will also choke him out and force him to eat trash."

Bizarrely, at one point, the parents tried to hand Adrian over to CPS but were told they'd be charged with abandonment, so they did not pursue that avenue. If it's true they were told that – why were they?

There were 32 surveillance cameras around the home, so that Adrian had no relief from his torture. It is hard not to use the word 'monsters' when discussing Adrian's murderers. If you can bear it, here is a list of some of the tortures this precious child endured.

- Plywood door across the shower, ensuring no escape. Adrian's lips became torn and bloody due to gnawing at the plywood, either in an attempt to escape or to feed himself on the wood
- When he could no longer stand, Adrian was tied to a chair in the shower stall
- Starved – locks and alarms on fridge and food cupboards
- Strapped to inversion table with weights on his ankles, which became hugely swollen
- Bound to cutting boards intended to make him stand totally upright, unable to relieve the pain in his limbs by moving
- Shocked with a taser for up to 20 seconds at a time
- Taunted with a plate of food, with restrained hands and a bar of soap shoved into his mouth
- Made to stand outside on cold, January nights in Kansas City, with hands bound behind his back and his only

'No, I think that's everything.'

'Right, I'll get started on making some biscuits. Adrian loves my shortbread; he eats it with ice cream.'

'Sounds lovely. You take care now, Heather. Great job with all these kids!'

'Bye, and thanks for stopping by.'

'Bye,' says the lady, her voice sounding faint as she walks out of the door.

Heather dashes to the shower stall. 'You coughed, you little fucker.'

There is ice cream later. But I don't get any. I've been blindfolded and strapped to the inversion board ever since the lady's car pulled away.

'I said "No" and I meant "No",' bellows Daddy down the phone.

A pause.

'Because I damned well say so.'

The other person is talking.

'Your useless daughter couldn't take care of them. Heather and me are doing a great job, so just butt the fuck out.'

Heather comes into the kitchen. 'Who is it, Mike?'

'That bloody interfering woman. Dainna's mother.'

'Tell her to fuck off.'

respite from thirst, a drink of water from a cup on the ground
- Forced to carry heavy Tiki garden torches round the yard
- Neck-deep in stagnant pool water outdoors for hours, including overnight

The cause of Adrian's death was starvation.

Heather and Michael Jones pleaded guilty to murder and both were sentenced to a life term of 25 years without parole for Adrian's death.

Heather Jones had claimed that she felt helpless to protect Adrian and herself from her husband, but photo and video evidence revealed instead that she was the main abuser, and she was handed down an additional five years and eight months prison time for two counts of child cruelty. She is incarcerated at Topeka Correctional Facility.

The last time Judy Conway saw her grandson is etched on her memory: "I was getting ready to leave and he wouldn't let go of my leg. I knelt down in front of him and he told me that he loved me and he wanted to go with me and I told him that I loved him and that I would always be there for him and I'd always keep him safe."

Adrian's grandmother says she has a recurring dream, where she points a gun at Heather and Michael Jones, wraps Adrian up in a blanket and rescues him from the house. "As we're walking away, he says to me, 'What took you so long, Nana?'" She knows it is too late to save Adrian, but in the years since his death, Judy Conway has battled to implement a new law to help protect other children.

I make it my practice not to show the children's ravaged bodies and terrified faces, and I will maintain that here. But if you have any uncertainties as to what being abused to death actually means, and how cold and callous the perpetrators can be, you may decide to view the images and short clips of Adrian that you can find online. Along with a warning that they may haunt you, as they do me, you will find them on several news sites, such as the UK's Daily Mail.

But others are suffering at this level right now. In Adrian's name – please be alert to child abuse.

My thanks to Rianna from the US,
Debbie from the US, and several others
for asking me to include Adrian's story in this book.

Rest Safely in Peace, Adrian

Homeschooling in the 21st Century

Adrian is yet another child who was 'homeschooled'.

Many children are lovingly and successfully homeschooled by parents who have their best interests at heart. But some are not, and they are hidden away, living in pain and terror.

When choosing children to write about, I don't deliberately seek out those who were homeschooled. Yet time and again, I discover part way through researching their story that they were either homeschooled from the start of their 'education' or removed from school following allegations of abuse.

Allowing an abused child to be removed from school, out of sight of those who could witness what is happening, and summon help for them, is akin to confining them to a prison cell with the person who has already been proven to be torturing them. I find that as baffling as it is barbaric.

In doing so, we make it ridiculously easy for abusers to torture their children. Why on earth are we doing this? Why do we condemn these innocents to a living hell?

In Kansas, the state in which Adrian lived, school attendance is compulsory for children aged 7 – 18. This can take place in public or private schools. Kansas does not regulate homeschooling, with the only requirement under state law, both now and at the time of Adrian's death, being that families:

• Register the homeschool as a non-accredited private school, by filling out and mailing a form giving its name and location and the name of the person maintaining records.

That's it. Not even the child's name has to be given. There is no cost to register, and it has to be done once only. Michael Jones registered the '*Jones' Academy*' on 17 July, 2012.

Any other aspects are recommendations only, and are not enforced, such as the completion of the same number of hours of instruction as those in public schools, using competent instructors, and the reporting of academic achievements.

Reflecting on her grandson being bound to chopping boards, and made to spend his nights either neck-deep in a filthy outdoor pool or locked in a shower stall, Judy Conway wants Kansas to adopt requirements that include background checks for those registering home schools and a flagging system for at-risk children. "All I want is some oversight and accountability".

I have read that some Kansas homeschool advocates see *additional regulations* as unnecessary and intrusive. My question is, in addition to what? There are *no regulations*.

Some cloud the issue by saying that Adrian's murder wasn't a result of home education, but was a result of abusive parents, as if believing that stating the obvious contributes to an intelligent debate that could prevent children from suffering.

With even the most basic homeschool oversight, however, Adrian might have been saved.

Judy Conway says: "We just want these kids to be protected". So far, her words, and that of advocates in favour of even the most minimal regulation, have fallen on deaf ears.

Rachel Coleman is the co-founder of the Coalition for Responsible Home Education, and was homeschooled by her college-educated mother. She outlines four main suggestions for regulation:

1. *Background checks for those registering homeschools, in the same way that licensed teachers undergo background checks.* This does not have to be rigorous, but our homeschooled children are surely as worthy of a good education as publicly schooled.

2. *A flagging system for homeschooled children when social services have been involved.* This can prevent abusive parents from removing their victims from sight, and just this regulation alone would be a game-changer for abused children.

3. *An annual academic assessment by a mandatory reporter in which students take a test or have a portfolio review.* Again, these do not have to be rigorous. In this way, the student is meeting, without their parents, a qualified person who can ask the child if they have any concerns. If the testing element is contentious to some, let's do it without the test, but at least **make sure the child is seen**.

4. *A requirement for homeschooled students to have the same medical exams as public school students, including hearing and dental checks.* Some abused homeschooled children are also subjected to medical neglect.

But even these simple safeguards face fierce opposition, and those who refuse any oversight are quick to claim that safeguarding implies criticism of homeschooling itself. One such person says: "We are eager to see child abuse deaths go down, but it's not going to be by *pounding on home schooling,*" escalating from the desire to protect children from abusive homeschoolers, to claiming that minimal safeguards equates to *pounding* homeschooling in all its forms.

Others claim that Adrian's story is an "*extreme outlier*" saying that "a *single, powerful case* shouldn't determine policy." This is a sad reflection on society in general, with most people thinking that each child murder by abusive caregivers is a rare aberration. Hence they appear to believe Adrian's is a single case, also saying: "Students who attend public school still can suffer abuse." But we know that already; we know that child abuse occurs in all settings, whether in public schools or home schools.

Like the commentators above, I imagine that many of us have been in a position where we don't have a solid argument, and turn to the smoke and mirrors technique to put those who are questioning us off the scent. In doing so, they fail to see that the assertion never was, nor ever should be, that all homeschooling is wrong. The point is simply to protect those children whose homeschooling caregivers abuse them. Sometimes to death.

(As I mentioned in Volume 1, I was homeschooled for a short while, and it was a reasonably positive experience for me. And for many loving parents and their fortunate children, homeschooling is absolutely the right choice to make.)

Adrian's Law

Judy Conway (now Walsh), Adrian's grandmother, fought for several years to protect children in Adrian's name, and on 21 May 2021, *Adrian's Law* was instituted.

The parts appertaining to Adrian decree that:

Adults who witness abuse must report child abuse or face criminal charges

In heart-breaking video footage from the CCTV cameras, we see a naked Adrian, having sneaked out of the shower stall, getting a bowl of water and then hiding from the relative who walks into the kitchen. Adrian knew this individual was not going to help or comfort him. Under the new law, this third adult in the household, Michael Jones' uncle, would have faced criminal charges, as he didn't report the abuse he surely witnessed.

Departments of Child and Family Services, and law enforcement officers conducting an abuse or neglect investigation, must make a visual observation of a child suspected of being abused, and report this clearly

Investigators can no longer shirk their responsibilities by merely *knocking at the door and then leaving* when no one answers. Additionally, they cannot take the guardian's word for it that the child is not at home. This should make a huge difference in protecting children.

A committee to oversee social services is also part of the overall bill.

In the words of Mark Dupree, district attorney for Wyandotte County, who spoke at the ceremony to implement the bill: "No more hiding our babies, our abused children."

This Volume has covered particularly contentious material. But as always, it is only ever about raising awareness and protecting children. Even when sharing information on issues such as religion and homeschooling, I hope you will understand my intentions, even if you do not agree with every word.

Many people say that Adrian's story is the most horrifying they have encountered. To me, some of the most distressing evidence of his torture is the video clip in which he is searching through piles of trash for something to eat, with Heather looking on and commenting, without a shred of empathy. Adrian's body is frail and his voice faint, and it shows his bewilderment. We are not often witnesses to a human being's utter desolation. And once again, I'd like to warn you that if you watch clips of Adrian, they may upset you.

There's another clip of Adrian in the yard, handcuffed and eating from a dish of applesauce on the ground. Heather is watching from the window with one of her other children. She shows contempt for Adrian and disgust that he would eat something covered in dirt and bugs. I guess she doesn't know how it feels to be starved to death.

I hope that in my writing of his story, I have done justice to this most precious little boy who was tortured with such unbelievable cruelty.

There are many other 'Adrians' out there right now. There are also many others who have suffered abuse and survived. These include some of my readers, many of whom have broken the cycle to become compassionate adults and loving parents. They have my utmost respect, and if you are one such person, I hope you know what an immense difference you are making, and that you are quite simply saving lives.

Please don't feel guilty if you 'enjoy' my books. Most people tell me they feel a mixture of emotions, and I'm glad you're amongst those who are willing to face the reality of the suffering taking place right under our noses.

Apathy ensures that the abusers win.

> And if you've been moved by the children's stories and found them interesting, I would greatly appreciate a star rating or review – these encourage me to keep writing, and help others to find my books.

This book is dedicated to the memory of

Max, Star, Shane,
Daniel, Hana and Adrian

Will You Help Me To Raise Awareness?

If you are able to spare a moment to rate or review, please do so in your usual way, or use the QR code or link to get back to the book's page:

mybook.to/Abused-To-Death-4

Then scroll waaay down

until you see Write a Review

(usually on the left side)

Your review or rating will help to spread awareness of abuse, and just a star rating or a few words is enough.

Join Us On Facebook

Want to connect with me and join a community of people who want to prevent child abuse?

I honour the murdered children on my Facebook page, and if you'd like to come and say 'Hi' on one of my posts, it'd be great to see you there.

If you wish, you can **Follow Me & Share** my posts.

Just scan this code:

Or use this link:

https://www.facebook.com/AbusedToDeath/

Or within Facebook, type into the search bar:

Jessica Jackson – Writer Against Abuse

Hello (again!) from Jess

Would you like to **join my Readers' List**, by picking up your free ebook overleaf?

And would you please do me a great favour?

*Because my books are so sad, I double-check that you want to join my Readers' List, and so you'll receive a quick email from me, to ask you to **confirm your place**.*

> *Can you please reply either **Yes or No** to this email? It only takes a few seconds but is **incredibly** helpful to me.*

If you don't receive the email almost instantly, please check Junk/Spam – I can't add you without your reply.

Thank you; I really appreciate this.

Readers' List Benefits

Members get special offers, along with each new release at the subscriber price. And if you'd like to be more involved, you can **suggest children to include**, give your input on cover design, and lots more.

> *I'm always interested in what my readers think, and so on the day after you've confirmed your place and joined us, I'll email you with the question:*
>
> *"ARE THEY MONSTERS?"*
>
> *I'd love to include your opinion in my readers' poll.*
>
> *Then I'll leave you in peace for a while!*

So, get your free ebook overleaf, and thank you in advance if you decide to join us.

Pick Up Your Free E-Book and Join Us!

Isaiah Torres was just six years old when he was abused to death in the most appalling way.

Pick up your copy of your free ebook

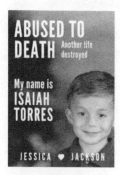

Just scan this code:

Or use this link:
https://BookHip.com/VNGMZJJ

Then be sure to click Yes or No on the quick email I'll send to confirm your place – it looks like this:

Yes thanks, I'd love to join, Jess

OR

No, I won't join just now, Jess

Find All My Books on Amazon

Find them in your usual way, or you can ...

Search Amazon for:

Abused To Death by Jessica Jackson

Or scan this code:

Or use this link:

viewbook.at/abused-series

If you wish, you can also Follow Me on Amazon.

Don't Miss A Thing

Pick up your free ebook:

Just scan this code:

https://BookHip.com/VNGMZJJ

Then click Yes or No on your confirmation email

Follow me on Facebook:

https://www.facebook.com/AbusedToDeath/

Follow me on Amazon:

viewbook.at/abused-series

*(Make sure Settings in **Communications Preferences in your Amazon account** are set to receive info about new releases.)*

Thank You For Reading Volume 4

I hope you have enjoyed reading this volume.

I'm aware that it covers some controversial issues, and I do not intend to offend anyone by alluding to the darker sides of homeschooling and religion. Both of these have played a positive part in my own life, so I feel I can appreciate their advantages as well as when twisted for malicious and cruel purposes.

I hope you'll continue to be with me as I write more children's stories and try to play my part in breaking the taboos that surround children murdered by abuse.

Thank you again for reading, and please get in touch if you feel as I do:

jessicajackson@jesstruecrime.com

Selected Resources

For Max, Star, Shane, Daniel, Hana & Adrian

The Playroom Maxwell Schollenberger, Pennsylvania, USA aged 12 Died 2020		• Trial begins for Kimberly Marie Maurer, accused in tortured death of Annville boy – Matthew Toth – Lebanon Daily News • Max Schollenberger's mother: "I thought Maxwell was in good hands" – Kim Strong – Lebanon Daily News • Dad's girlfriend on trial over neglect, starvation death of 12-year-old – Jonathan Bergmueller – jbergmueller@pennlive.com
Falling Star Star Hobson West Yorkshire, UK aged 1 Died 2020		• Heartbreaking photo shows bruised Star Hobson months before she was killed – Andy Wells, Yahoo News, 15.12.21 • CPS.gov.uk – 14.12.21 • Mother and partner guilty over death of 16-month-old Star Hobson – Youtube clip from ITV news https://www.youtube.com/watch?v=y9ccsEDFkXs
If You Tell Shane Watson Washington, USA aged 18 or 19 Died 1994		• If You Tell – Gregg Olsen – Thomas & Mercer 2019 • There is evil among us – Andrea Cavallier – Daily Mail 29 April 2023 • Kids of murderer Michelle 'Shelly' Knotek warn their mom could kill again – NYPost.com – Jane Ridley – 30 November 2019
Greedy Daniel Pelka Coventry, UK aged 4 Died 2012		• Sibling hid food for starved boy – bbc.co.uk – 31.07.13 • Lessons to be Learnt – Daniel Pelka – Staffordshire SCB & Stoke-on-Trent SCB – 2013 • Killer stepfather of schoolboy Daniel Pelka found dead in prison – Helen Pidd – theguardian.com – 29.01.16
Murder By The Book Hana Befekadu Williams Washington, USA aged 13 Died 2011		• poundpuplegacy.org – exposing the dark side of adoption – Hana and Immanuel Williams • https://www.dailymail.co.uk/Hana-Williams – Washington-adoptive-parents-Larry-Carri-Williams-GUILTY-manslaughter • Society's Child – Sign of the Times Jeff Hodson – Seattle Times – Mon, 07 Nov 2011 • To Train Up A Child – Michael and Debi Pearl – Published 1994 / 2015 by No Greater Joy Ministries
The Pig-Pen Adrian Jones Kansas City, USA aged 7 Died 2015		• "My Daddy keeps hitting me in the head" – dailymail.com – 11 May 2017 – Martin Gould and Jennifer Smith • Surveillance footage captures last days of tortured KCK boy's life – Action News – kshb.com – 04 May 2017 – Jessica McMaster • Adrian's Law – kslegislature.org – Housebill 2158 – 2021 • Katie Moore – Topeka Capital-Journal, with contributions by Capital-Journal staff writer Angela Deines • https://www.thesun.co.uk/news/3525009/adrian-jones-shocked-stun-gun-dad-michael-jailed/

Disclaimer

My aim is to tell stories of murdered children with a combination of accuracy and readability, to heighten awareness of child torture and murder, and to explore ways of preventing further tragedies. I have relied on the factual information available to me during my research, and where I have added characters or dramatised events to better tell the child's story, I believe I have done so without significantly altering the important details. If anyone has further information about the children, particularly if you knew them and have anecdotes to share about their life, I would be delighted to hear from you. Likewise, whilst every attempt has been made to make contact with copyright holders, if I have unwittingly used any material when I was not at liberty to do so, please contact me so that this can be rectified at:

jessicajackson@jesstruecrime.com

Made in the USA
Las Vegas, NV
05 September 2024